MAKING BUYING DECISIONS

Making Buying Decisions

Using the Computer as a Tool
Second Edition

Richard Clodfelter
University of South Carolina

Fairchild Publications, Inc.
New York

Executive Editor: Olga T. Kontzias

Assistant Acquisitions Editor: Carolyn Purcell

Editor: Joann Muscolo

Assistant Production Editor: Amy Zarkos

Art Director: Adam B. Bohannon

Production Manager: Priscilla Taguer

Editorial Assistant: Suzette Lam

Copy Editor: Donna Frasetto

Proofreader: Roberta Mantus

Interior Design: Charles B. Hames

Cover Design: Adam B. Bohannon

Library of Congress Catalog Card Number: 2002103893

ISBN: 1-56367-223-5

GST R 133004424

Printed in the United States of America

Table of Contents

Extended Table of Contents

Preface

This workbook is designed to help you develop a facility with numbers that will help you make better retail buying decisions. Through carefully constructed lessons you will:

- Learn mathematical calculations used by retail buyers.
- Learn fundamental computerized spreadsheet skills.
- Apply mathematical formulas to create useful spreadsheets.
- Develop a portfolio of spreadsheet files useful on the job.

MATH AND COMPUTERS: CRITICAL TOOLS FOR THE MARKETPLACE

Planning for a career in retailing requires that you develop effective merchandising skills, including merchandise knowledge, familiarity with markets and customers, and strong negotiating skills. Fundamental to your success as a professional, however, is your facility with the computations that reflect the profit-driven dimension of business. Mathematical and computational skills are crucial as you develop planning strategies that will provide adequate quantities of merchandise to your customers at prices they are willing to pay.

Too often, merchandising students are not comfortable working with numbers. Many times, the classes that you may have taken stressed only rote memorization of merchandising formulas. But, in today's workplace, merchandisers and buyers are working with numbers in entirely different ways. No longer are they performing tedious and repetitious math calculations. Instead, professionals spend their time reading and interpreting computer printouts as well as constructing and using computerized spreadsheets that will allow them to perform repetitive calculations quickly.

Today, it is almost inconceivable that anyone involved in merchandising does not have daily contact with a computer. Computers have become so affordable and essential that they are being used by small as well as large retailers. By reducing the time needed to perform mathematical calculations, merchandisers and buyers are able to spend more of their time making sounder purchasing decisions that will favorably affect the store's operating efficiency and profitability.

You must also realize that computers cannot solve all your problems. As a planning tool, the computer is only as effective as the person inputting information and instructions. If incorrect data are input into the computer, the results will be incorrect.

Buyers and merchandisers must possess a general knowledge of computers and how to manipulate data, especially through the use of spreadsheets. You probably have already taken a computer course, but did you learn specific applications related to your career objective in retailing? Too often, the answer is no. The exercises in this workbook are designed to incorporate computer training with learning the fundamental mathematical concepts used in merchandising.

USE WITH OTHER TEXTS

This workbook is designed to *supplement* other textbooks in merchandising, retail mathematics, retail buying, and retail management/ strategy courses. In the Fairchild series, it could easily be used to more fully develop merchandising concepts presented in *Retail Buying*.

APPROACH AND FORMAT OF THE WORKBOOK

In this workbook, merchandising concepts are presented in a simple, understandable way that minimizes rote memorization of formulas. Activities involve solving merchandising problems by using computerized spreadsheets. You will also observe how less time is needed to perform repetitive calculations; and, by constructing and using spreadsheets for each mathematical operation, you will develop a better understanding of the merchandising concepts being studied.

Mathematical concepts used in merchandising are presented in 11 problem areas. Each one contains the following sections:

- The merchandising concept being presented is reviewed.
- A sample problem with its solution is presented for each concept.
- Problems are included for use with spreadsheets that have already been prepared. These spreadsheets require that you substitute designated variables to answer "what if?" The purpose of these problems is to show you the ease with which mathematical calculations can be made using the computer.
- Additional assignments are presented for you to use with spreadsheets that *you design*. For problems in the first several chapters, a step-by-step process will be detailed for constructing the spreadsheet. For later chapters, you will have the opportunity to design the entire spreadsheet based on the problems presented.
- The **Glossary** and **Appendix** serve as ready reference tools as you complete the projects in this book.

Upon completing the exercises and assignments in this workbook, you should have a more genuine understanding of mathematical concepts used in merchandising as well as increased familiarity with computer operations. Above all, once you have completed this workbook you will have a disk filled with spreadsheet applications that you can carry with you into your retailing career upon graduation.

Acknowledgements

To the reviewers who examined the text and offered suggestions for its improvement, the author is most appreciative. Reviewers included: Tana Stufflebean, Rose E. Bednarz, June Fischer, Cynthia Jasper, Celia Stall-Meadows, Michele Granger, Luann Goskil, Li Zhang.

Finally, the author is especially grateful to Mary McGarry and Joann Muscolo, editors at Fairchild, for their guidance and encouragement in this project.

MAKING BUYING DECISIONS

Chapter 1

Using Computerized Spreadsheets

In this workbook you will be performing mathematical calculations using a computerized *spreadsheet*, an electronic worksheet. A *Merchandising Compact Disk (CD)* accompanies this workbook and contains many spreadsheets that have already been prepared with *Microsoft Excel*. You will use the files on this CD to solve problems in the workbook. You will also design and construct your own spreadsheets and store them on the disk.

Spreadsheets can be used to perform a simple operation such as adding two numbers, or calculations can involve hundreds of interrelated entries. More significant than performing mathematical calculations on spreadsheets, you can quickly make recalculations by changing one or several of the numbers that you have entered or by changing formulas. Using the speed of computers, spreadsheet programs allow you to make repetitive and tedious mathematical calculations quickly and efficiently.

A spreadsheet can be thought of as a long, rectangular sheet of paper divided into smaller rectangles, called *cells*. You can type words or numbers in these rectangles, or you can type formulas that can add, subtract, multiply, or divide numbers in whatever combination you choose.

Spreadsheets are invaluable tools for retail buyers and managers when they are developing "what if" strategies. For example, after formulas have been set up, you may want to enter one set of numbers to estimate sales. Just as quickly, you can enter another set of numbers to estimate sales for a different scenario. You could keep doing this for as many sets of numbers as you desire. Performing repetitive mathematical calculations and "what if" analyses are what spreadsheets do best.

BASIC COMPUTER OPERATIONS

Now you should be ready to see what a spreadsheet looks like on the computer. Follow the instructions listed below to load the spreadsheet program, select the data drive, and open a file.

Loading Files from the *Merchandising CD*

1. Start your computer.
2. Insert the *Merchandising CD* into your CD-ROM.
3. Open *Microsoft Excel* on your computer and use the **File** menu to open drive D.
4. A directory of the *Merchandising CD* appears as shown in Figure 1.1. Notice that files are titled by lesson for easy reference.

Opening a File

1. Use the mouse to highlight the file name **CH01** and press **Open** or double-click your mouse.
2. You should now be able to see a part of the spreadsheet on your computer screen as shown in Figure 1.2.

Reading the Spreadsheet Screen

On the spreadsheet the ***highlight bar*** identifies the current cell. You will also notice letters across the top of the screen. They identify a vertical series of cells in a ***column***. Numbers can be seen on the left side of your computer screen. They are used to identify horizontal series of cells in a ***row***. Spreadsheet programs usually contain more rows and columns than you will need in your calculations.

Each cell on the spreadsheet also has an address that is shown on the status line of the screen. The ***cell address*** is determined by its column and row location. For example, the cell in the upper left corner

FIGURE 1.1

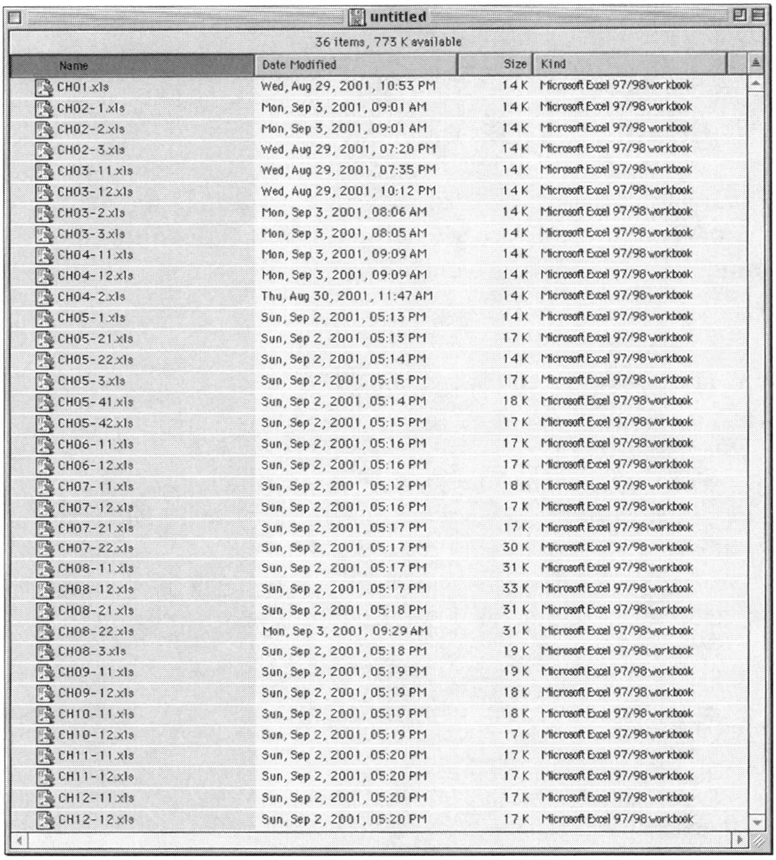

of the spreadsheet has an address of A1. The cell is located in column A, row 1. You can move to other cells in the spreadsheet by using the mouse.

Both text and numbers can be entered into a cell, but with numbers you must designate how you want your data presented (e.g., number of decimal places, currency). Using the **Format** command on the menu will allow you to change how numbers are displayed in any cell, row, or column.

You must follow mathematical rules as you work with spreadsheets. Formulas are calculated in normal mathematical order. *Operations inside parentheses are performed first, followed by multiplication, division, addition, and then subtraction.*

FIGURE 1.2

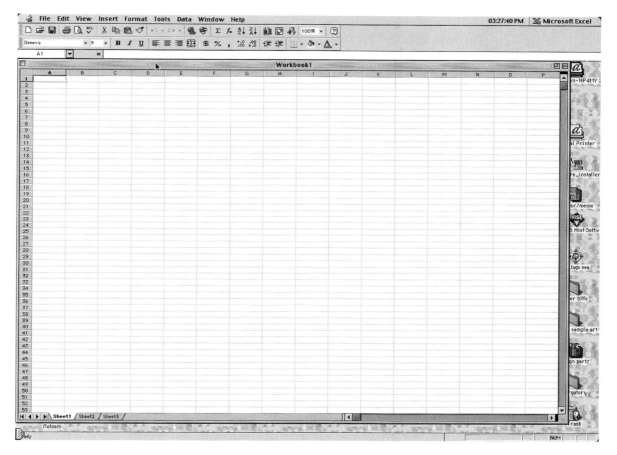

Changing the Width of a Column

If, after performing any calculation, the symbol "#####" appears, the cell is not large enough to display the data; but you can easily enlarge the column to accommodate the data. The width of the column in which data are to be entered or displayed can also be made smaller, if desired.

To change the width of a column:

1. With your mouse move your cursor to the top of the spreadsheet where columns are identified as A, B, C, and so on. With the cursor, highlight the line to the right of the column that you wish to adjust. The cursor changes appearance when it is positioned correctly.

2. Hold down your mouse button. Drag the mouse to make the column the correct width.

Changing How Numbers Are Displayed

You can also use commands under the **Format** menu to designate how data in a specific cell, row, or column are to be presented. You can display the data as whole numbers, dollars (currency), or decimals. You can also designate how many decimal places you wish to use.

To change how values are displayed:

1. Highlight the cell you wish to change, or highlight the cells in the row(s) or column(s) you wish to change.
2. Use commands listed under the **Format** menu to change how your data will be presented.

Entering Formulas

Formulas calculate a value based on the values in other cells of the spreadsheet. In fact, a formula can include any cell on the spreadsheet. You can also combine mathematical operations–for example, A1 + (A2 − A3)/A4. Remember that *before any formula can be entered, the "=" sign must be typed first.*

To enter a formula:

1. Click the cell where the result of the formula will appear.
2. Type the "=" sign. Now type the formula. For example, if you want to add the values in cells A1, A2, and A3, type **A1 + A2 + A3** after the "=" sign. You could also click the cell of the value that you are adding. For the formula presented, you could click cell A1, then type the "+" sign, then click cell A2 and type "+", and finally click cell A3.
3. When you have finished entering a formula, press **ENTER,** which indicates to the computer that you have completed your formula.
4. Your results will appear in the cell where you entered the formula if data were in the other cells.

Functions, abbreviated formulas that perform a specific operation on a group of values, can also be used to save time. For example, the **SUM** function is a shortcut for entering a formula that adds numbers.

SUM automatically adds numbers in a range. For example, if you wanted to add the numbers in cells A1 through A3, you could simply type **=SUM (A1:A3).**

MERCHANDISING CONCEPT 1–1: INPUT DATA AND INTERPRET COMPUTER OUTPUT

Retail buyers and managers must be able to input data on spreadsheet programs and interpret the output they receive. You should now be ready to observe exactly what computerized spreadsheets can do. On the screen you are viewing, you should see that some text has already been entered. In addition, one formula has also been entered.

PRACTICE ACTIVITIES

The activities that follow will allow you to become comfortable entering data, performing mathematical calculations, and interpreting output. These activities begin with a quick review of decimals and percentages. Correct answers to the exercises can be found at the end of this chapter.

Activity 1: Review Decimals and Percentages

When working with spreadsheets, many students have difficulty with percentages and decimals. In most word-problem situations, many numbers are stated as percentages. Before you can enter them onto a spreadsheet, they must be expressed as a decimal. In addition, many of the figures that you will read on a computer screen will be displayed as a decimal. You will need to express them as percentages or dollars and cents. Here is a quick review of this concept.

> The term *percent* means "per hundred"; thus, 11 percent means 11 per hundred, or 0.11.
>
> $11\% = 11/100 = 0.11$

When expressing a percentage as a decimal, move the decimal two places to the left and drop the percent sign. For example, 5 percent would be entered as .05; .5 percent would be entered as .005, and 55.5 percent would be entered as .555.

The numbers that follow appear in word problems that you will be solving using a spreadsheet. Express each of them as a decimal. Correct responses are presented at the end of this chapter.

1. 1%
2. 1.5%
3. 100%
4. 150%
5. 47.8%
6. 52.0%
7. .4%
8. 10%
9. 10.4%
10. 3.1%

When the computer makes calculations for you, the numbers will be expressed as decimals just as they are when you use your calculator. Usually, you will need to *round* these numbers for the situation with which you are working. For example, 1.643456 would be expressed as $1.64 if your answer should be in dollars and cents, or as 164.3 percent if your answer should be a percentage. You can also use the **Format** menu command to change how data are displayed.

With dollars, you will need to express your answer to two decimal places, and, with most percentages, you will need to express them to one decimal place, or tenths of a percent. (*Note*: Rounding rules vary, but "rounding off" is the most common method. Round *up* if the number to the right of the one you are rounding is 5 or more; round *down* if it is less than 5.) When expressing percentages as decimals, express them to the nearest tenth of a percent as shown in the preceding example.

When you are solving problems in this workbook, numbers similar to the ones that follow could be displayed on your computer screen. Express each of them as dollars and cents, rounding off to the nearest cent.

11. 64.3214987
12. 8.238765
13. 581.234567
14. .89543453
15. 45677.23765

When you are solving problems in this workbook, numbers in decimal form, similar to the ones that follow, could be displayed on your computer screen. Express each of these decimals as a percentage *rounded off to the nearest tenth of a percent.*

16. 6.44453
17. 33.3333
18. 67.7777
19. .056742
20. .002876

Activity 2: Enter Data and Calculate

1. Move to cell B3 on the spreadsheet found on **CH01** that requires sales data for Quarter 1 of Year 1.
2. Input **$35,000** and press **ENTER**.
3. Use your mouse to move to cell B4, input **$37,000**, and press **ENTER**.
4. Move to cell B5 and enter **$36,000**. Enter **$21,000** in cell B6.
5. The formula to calculate total sales for Year 1 has already been entered in cell B7, and you made recalculations with each number that you input.

Activity 3: Revise Data and Recalculate

After calculating total sales for Year 1, you realize that the sales figure you entered for Quarter 4 was incorrect.

1. Move to cell B6 and erase the data already in the cell. Highlight the value in the cell and press the **Delete** key.
2. Input **$38,000** and press **ENTER**.
3. Total sales have been recalculated.

Activity 4: Create a Formula to Add Numbers

Now you will need to set up a formula that will calculate total sales for Year 2. Because you want to calculate the total of the quarterly sales figures, there are two different ways you can express the formula. First, type "=" in the cell; then type **C3 + C4 + C5 + C6**. Or, you could type **SUM (C3:C6)** after typing the "=" sign. The second formula directs the computer to add (SUM) all the numbers in the cells between C3 and C6. The ":" designates *all* the numbers between the two numbers listed. Also, you could click the mouse on the cell that you wish to be a part of your formula. For example, after typing "=", click the mouse on cell C3, type the "+" sign, click the mouse on cell C4, type the "+" sign, click the mouse on cell C5, type the "+" sign, and click the mouse on cell C6.

1. Move to cell C7. Type either formula described above and press **EN-TER**.
2. Enter the following sales data for Year 2:

Quarter 1	$40,000
Quarter 2	$46,000
Quarter 3	$45,000
Quarter 4	$50,000

Activity 5: Create a Formula to Calculate Percentage of Change Between Two Numbers

After examining the data, you want to determine by what percentage quarterly sales changed from Year 1 to Year 2. Mathematically, this requires finding the difference in sales for each quarter and dividing by quarterly sales for the *first* year, as the following formula indicates:

$$\frac{\text{(Second Year's Quarterly Sales} - \text{First Year's Quarterly Sales)}}{\text{First Year's Quarterly Sales}}$$

For the first quarter, this calculation would be:

$$(40,000 - 35,000)/35,000 = 0.14285$$

Spreadsheets can be used to quickly perform calculations such as these. Just substitute the cell addresses for the values you wish to calculate. For the first quarter, the spreadsheet formula would be:

$$(C3 - B3)/B3$$

Closely examine this formula. The parentheses indicate that mathematical calculations inside the parentheses would be performed first; otherwise, the data in C3 would be divided by B3, which is not what you want. The formula specifies that the data in cell B3 will be subtracted from the data in cell C3. Then this difference will be divided by the data in cell B3.

FIGURE 1.3

	Sales Year 1	Sales Year 2	% Change
Quarter 1	$35,000.00	$40,000.00	14.3%
Quarter 2	$37,000.00	$46,000.00	24.3%
Quarter 3	$36,000.00	$45,000.00	25.0%
Quarter 4	$38,000.00	$50,000.00	31.6%
TOTALS	$146,000.00	$181,000.0	24.0%

Now you are ready to label the column and enter the formulas to calculate the quarterly percentage changes.

1. Move to cell D2. The percentage changes will be displayed in column D for each quarter.
2. Type **% Change** and press **ENTER**. Now, you are ready to enter the formulas to perform the required calculations. You will need to establish five formulas–one for each of the quarters, as well as one for the Totals row.
3. Move to cell D3 for the first quarter. Type **(C3 − B3)/B3** and press **ENTER**. You will notice that your answer is expressed as a decimal. Use the **Format** menu command to display your data with one decimal place.
4. Now, set up formulas that will calculate the percentage changes for Quarters 2, 3, and 4, and for the yearly totals.
5. Your screen should resemble Figure 1.3.

Activity 6: Revise Data and Recalculate

To illustrate the speed with which recalculations can be made, replace the sales data that you have entered for Year 1.

1. Erase the sales data in cells B3 through B6 and replace them with the data below.

	Year 1
Quarter 1	$30,000
Quarter 2	$31,000
Quarter 3	$32,000
Quarter 4	$30,000

FIGURE 1.4

	Sales Year 1	Sales Year 2	% Change
Quarter 1	$30,000.00	$40,000.00	33.3%
Quarter 2	$31,000.00	$46,000.00	48.4%
Quarter 3	$32,000.00	$45,000.00	40.6%
Quarter 4	$30,000.00	$50,000.00	66.7%
TOTALS	$123,000.00	$181,000.00	47.2%

2. You now have sales totals as well as percentages, which are based on your *new* sales figures, as shown in Figure 1.4.

ADDITIONAL COMPUTER OPERATIONS

This spreadsheet contains other commands that can be used later in this workbook as you create your own spreadsheets. These commands involve editing and saving your work, printing, and quitting. Steps to perform these computer operations are described next.

Using Edit Commands

What happens when you find you need a column between two that you have already created? Do you have to start over? What happens when you need to erase all the input in a specific column? Do you have to go to each cell and use the backspace key? What should you do when you need the same heading on two rows? Do you have to type the heading twice?

No is the answer to all these questions if you learn some of the other special commands on the spreadsheet.

Using the **Insert** menu command allows you to add empty rows or columns to any spreadsheet that you have already created. To insert a row or column: Highlight the column *to the right* of where the new column is to be added to add a blank column. To add a blank row, highlight the row *below* where the new row is to be located.

Te erase data in several cells, highlight all the cells that contain data to be deleted. Press the **Delete** key. If you make a mistake, click the **Undo** command.

Using the **Copy** command (under the **Edit** menu command) allows you to copy the content of a cell, column, or row and place it in another location on the spreadsheet. To copy a cell, row, or column, highlight the values to be copied. Press **Copy**. Move the cursor to the location (cell, row, or column) where you want the information copied. Highlight that area and press **Paste**.

You may want to practice these operations using the file on which you are working. However, you should save the file under a different name, as explained in the next section.

Saving Your Work

Any time you want to stop working on your computer, you will need to go to the **File** menu to save your work. You should save your work *under a different file name* so that you will always have the original lesson file for reference. Simply add an **A** (for answer) to the lesson file name when you save.

To save your Chapter 1 file as a separate answer file:

1. Choose **Save As** from the **File** menu.
2. At the cursor type **CH01A** and select the drive to which you will be saving the file. Press **ENTER**. Note that the open document keeps its original file name.

Printing

In each chapter of this workbook, you will find forms on which to record your answers for specific assignments. Record information from your computer screen on these forms, or your instructor may require that you print each screen.

To print the file you have been working on:

1. Check to ensure that a printer is connected to your computer.
2. Choose **Print** from the **File** menu.
3. Press **ENTER**. The file will be sent to your printer.

Quitting

When you want to stop work, first save your work. Then, close the file and quit the spreadsheet:

1. Choose **Close** from the **File** menu.
2. If you have not already saved your document, a message will appear asking if the current document needs to be saved.
3. Remove the *Merchandising CD* from drive D and shut down your computer.

When you have completed the assignments in this workbook, you will have spreadsheet applications that you can use for the merchandising calculations most frequently performed by buyers. If you need other calculations, you should be able to design your own spreadsheets with little difficulty. Although *Microsoft Excel* is used for spreadsheets in this workbook, almost all spreadsheet programs operate in a similar manner.

ANSWERS TO CHAPTER ACTIVITIES

Activity 1

1. .01	8. .1	15. $45,677.24
2. .015	9. .104	16. 644.5%
3. 1.0	10. .031	17. 3333.3%
4. 1.5	11. $64.32	18. 6777.8%
5. .478	12. $8.24	19. 5.7%
6. .52	13. $581.23	20. .3%
7. .004	14. $.90	

Activity 2
Total Sales for Year 1: $129,000

Activity 3
Total Sales for Year 1: $146,000

Activity 4
Total Sales for Year 2: $181,000

Activity 5

	% Change
Quarter 1	14.3%
Quarter 2	24.3%
Quarter 3	25.0%
Quarter 4	31.6%
Totals	24.0%

Activity 6

Total Sales for Year 1: $123,000

	% Change
Quarter 1	33.3%
Quarter 2	48.4%
Quarter 3	40.6%
Quarter 4	66.7%
Totals	47.2%

Chapter 2

Individual Markups

MERCHANDISING CONCEPT 2–1:
CALCULATE RETAIL PRICE

The goal of every retail store is to make a profit; however, achieving profits requires the careful planning and control of all business activities. Well-planned merchandising activities will be crucial to any retail business earning a profit–the right merchandise must be purchased and offered at a price customers are willing to pay. One of the most important tasks facing retailers is establishing retail prices. That price must reflect market conditions and cover the store's operating expenses while yielding the desired profit. Moreover, the retail price must be attractive to customers.

In this workbook, you will start with some of the basic pricing calculations and steadily move to more advanced merchandising activities. As you learn how one item is priced, the same concepts will apply to all the merchandise that any store will handle. The difference between the retailer's cost and the selling price is the *markup*, which is graphically illustrated in Figure 2.1. The term *individual markup* is used to describe markup on only *one* item and can be calculated using a simple formula:

Individual Markup = Unit Retail Price − Unit Cost

Retailers must constantly monitor markups to ensure that they are covering all the store's operating expenses and providing the desired

FIGURE 2.1

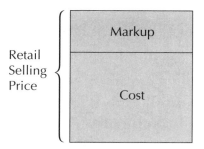

profit. At many stores, a ***markup percentage*** is calculated and used on all merchandise in a particular department or product classification.

Once the buyer or store owner has negotiated the cost of merchandise with the vendor, the desired markup percentage can be used to calculate the retail price that should be placed on the items. The following formula can be used for this calculation:

Retail = Cost/(100% − Markup %)

SAMPLE PROBLEM

A buyer purchases men's shirts for $12 each. If a 45-percent markup is used, what should be the retail price of each shirt?
Sample Solution

Retail = Cost/(100% − Markup %)
Retail = $12/(100% − 45%)
Retail = $12/(.55)
Retail = $21.82

By using the formula, the buyer has determined that a retail price of $21.82 must be placed on this item if a 45 percent markup is to be achieved. The buyer, however, may select a retail price that better fits the price lines in the store for that product category, such as $21.89, $21.99, or $22.00. If the buyer prices the item below $21.82, the desired markup will not be realized; but, as you will learn later, other items may be priced above their calculated retail price, while some others may be priced lower. In the final analysis, retailers are most concerned about achieving the desired markup on *total sales*, not just the sale of one item.

FIGURE 2.2

Calculating Retail Price	
Cost	$12.00
Markup	0.45
Retail	$21.82

Using Computerized Spreadsheets

Calculating the retail prices on hundreds of individual items is a tedious process. A computerized spreadsheet can be used to calculate individual retail prices very quickly. Follow the instructions listed below to solve the sample problem that you just examined.

1. Place the *Merchandising CD* in drive D and load *Microsoft Excel.*
2. Select and open file **CH02-1** from drive D.
3. In cell B4, type **12** (the dollar cost of one shirt in the example above) and press **ENTER**.
4. In cell B5, type **.45** (the decimal equivalent of a 45% markup) and press **ENTER**.
5. Because a formula has already been entered, the computer has calculated the retail price. To check the accuracy of your data input, examine Figure 2.2. Use this spreadsheet to calculate the retail price for each of the items listed on **ASSIGNMENT 2.1**. Before entering any information in a cell, make sure that any previous entries have been erased. Record all your answers on the form provided.
6. When you have completed the lesson, **Save** the file under the file name **CH02-1A**, and then **Close** the file.
7. **Quit** the spreadsheet, unless you will be completing the next assignment immediately.

ASSIGNMENT 2.1

Calculating Retail Price

Your department has just received 20 different items in a shipment from Acme Inc. The unit cost of each item is listed on page 21. Calculate the retail price for each item based on a 43.7 percent individual markup.

	Unit Cost	Unit Retail
1.	$15.50	
2.	$17.50	
3.	$28.00	
4.	$10.90	
5.	$11.00	
6.	$10.00	
7.	$6.50	
8.	$17.75	
9.	$18.00	
10.	$17.25	
11.	$5.84	
12.	$4.93	
13.	$6.63	
14.	$22.63	
15.	$10.50	
16.	$5.99	
17.	$9.99	
18.	$19.55	
19.	$22.50	
20.	$37.09	

MERCHANDISING CONCEPT 2–2: CALCULATE DESIRED COST

Buyers often purchase items with a specific retail price in mind. If buyers have a good understanding of their customers' buying habits, they can examine merchandise in the market and determine whether or not their customers would feel that the required retail price would be reasonable. In such situations, buyers will want to calculate the desired cost of an item *before* going to market or consulting with vendors. Buyers may only want to consider merchandise that is being sold at a cost near the one they have calculated.

Cost can be calculated using the following formula:

$$\textbf{Cost} = \textbf{Retail} \times (\textbf{100\%} - \textbf{Markup \%})$$

SAMPLE PROBLEM

Joan Anderson is a buyer for lamps. She wants to add a new line of lamps to the department's inventory. She feels that customers will be

willing to pay $70 for the lamps. If a 45 percent markup is needed, what cost should Joan seek when visiting the market next week?
Sample Solution

Cost = Retail × (100% − Markup %)
Cost = $70 × (100% − 45%)
Cost = $70 × (.55)
Cost = $38.50

Joan would need to locate vendors who were selling lamps at approximately $38.50. However, no vendor may be selling lamps at this price. Joan may decide to purchase the lamps and readjust the planned retail price once the lamps are in the store, or she may decide not to purchase the lamps if the resulting retail price is higher than she feels customers will pay.

Using Computerized Spreadsheets

A computerized spreadsheet can also be used to quickly calculate desired costs for individual items. Follow the instructions listed below to solve the sample problem that you just examined.

1. Place the *Merchandising CD* in drive D and load *Miscrosoft Excel*.
2. Select and open file **CH02-2** from drive D.
3. Using the numbers presented in the sample problem, enter the retail price and the markup percentage.
4. Because a formula has already been entered, the computer has calculated the cost. To check the accuracy of your data input, examine Figure 2.3. Use the spreadsheet to calculate the desired cost for each of the

FIGURE 2.3

Calculating Cost	
Cost	$38.50
Markup	0.45
Retail	$70.00

items listed in **ASSIGNMENT 2.2**. Before entering any information in a cell, make sure that any previous entries have been erased. Record all your answers on the form provided.

5. When you have completed the lesson, **Save** the file under the file name **CH02-2A**, and then **Close** the file.

6. **Quit** the spreadsheet, unless you will be completing the next assignment immediately.

ASSIGNMENT 2.2

Calculating Costs

You are planning to make a market visit next week and want to add several new items to your department's inventory. After examining customer needs, you have planned a unit retail price for each of these new items. Based on a 43.7 percent markup, what would be the desired cost of each item listed in the following chart?

	Unit Retail	Unit Cost
1.	$6.99	
2.	$6.49	
3.	$6.29	
4.	$6.79	
5.	$5.99	
6.	$10.00	
7.	$6.50	
8.	$17.75	
9.	$18.00	
10.	$17.25	
11.	$12.29	
12.	$4.95	
13.	$21.59	
14.	$22.69	
15.	$10.50	
16.	$1.49	
17.	$9.99	
18.	$19.29	
19.	$22.59	
20.	$37.00	

MERCHANDISING CONCEPT 2–3:
CALCULATE INDIVIDUAL MARKUP PERCENTAGE

As you have seen, the most basic component of pricing is markup, which is the difference between merchandise cost and its selling price. You have also learned that the markup that is established must *cover all operating expenses for a business or department* in addition to *providing a reasonable profit*. Of course, the actual sale price may be below the targeted price, so the actual markup is determined when an item is sold. Although it is important to know the dollar amount of markup, it is usually more important to know the markup percentage. Usually retailers state performance goals for a store or department in percentage terms rather than in dollars. Also, when making comparisons, dollar figures are usually not very meaningful.

Almost all retailers calculate markup as a percentage of retail price. In other words, they base their markups on the retail or selling price. Because profits are not realized until sales are made, it seems reasonable to base markups on selling price rather than the cost of an item. Basing markup percentages on retail selling price is also a standard practice of retail trade associations when they report industry statistics. In order to make comparisons with these reports, retailers must also base their markups on retail.

The markup percentage is calculated by first determining the dollar markup on an item, which is found by subtracting the cost of the item from its retail price. The dollar markup is then divided by the retail price. All these components are expressed in the following formula:

$$\text{Markup \%} = (\text{Retail} - \text{Cost})/\text{Retail}$$

SAMPLE PROBLEM

An item cost a retailer $56.32. If it sold for $112.00, what was the markup percentage?

Sample Solution

Markup % = (Retail − Cost)/Retail
Markup % = ($112 − $56.32)/$112
Markup % = $55.68/$112
Markup % = .4971428
Markup % = 49.7%

Using Computerized Spreadsheets

For all the calculations you have already made, you have simply input data onto spreadsheets that had been previously prepared. Once a spreadsheet has been constructed, it can be used over and over to perform repetitive mathematical calculations. Your task for this assignment is to construct a spreadsheet following specific instructions. In later chapters of the text, you will be asked to design spreadsheets without detailed instructions being presented, so be sure you understand each step. Follow these instructions:

1. Place the *Merchandising CD* in drive D and load *Microsoft Excel*.
2. Select and open file **CH02-3** from drive D.
3. Type all your titles first. Press **ENTER** after typing each word.
   - In cell A1, type **Calculating Markup Percentage**. Adjust the width of the column as needed.
   - In cell A3, type **Cost**.
   - In cell A4, type **Markup %**.
   - In cell A5, type **Retail**.
4. Now, you are ready to enter the formula that will perform the calculation to find the markup percentage. Move to cell B4 and type the "=" sign. Then, type **(B5 − B3)/B5**, which corresponds to the formula for calculating markup percentage. **Format** the cell to show only two decimal places. A sample screen appears in Figure 2.4.
5. Now complete the problems in **ASSIGNMENT 2.3**. Before entering any information in a cell, make sure that any previous entries have been erased. Record all your answers on the form.
6. When you have completed the lesson, **Save** the file under the file name **CH02-3A**, and then **Close** the file.
7. **Quit** the spreadsheet, unless you will be completing the next assignment immediately.

FIGURE 2.4

Calculating Markup Percentage	
Cost	$6.00
Markup %	52.0%
Retail	$12.50

ASSIGNMENT 2.3

Calculating Markup Percentages

Calculate the individual markup percentages for the following items:

	Unit Cost	Unit Retail	Markup Percentage
1.	$6.00	$12.50	
2.	$19.55	$38.79	
3.	$25.00	$55.00	
4.	$15.50	$38.00	
5.	$17.50	$48.00	
6.	$28.00	$48.00	
7.	$10.90	$21.50	
8.	$6.75	$13.00	
9.	$4.00	$8.00	
10.	$4.50	$9.75	
11.	$15.00	$35.00	
12.	$16.50	$21.75	
13.	$39.73	$68.50	
14.	$40.00	$58.00	
15.	$6.00	$7.80	
16.	$4.56	$12.15	
17.	$7.80	$12.00	
18.	$60.00	$90.00	
19.	$70.00	$95.20	
20.	$18.00	$30.00	

SUMMARY AND REVIEW

Buyers will use calculations such as markup to continually monitor the store or department's performance for a specified period of time. They will compare there figures against (1) established goals, (2) past records for the department or store, or (3) industry averages. Average markup percentages for some specific product categories are presented in Figure 2.5. Current industry averages are available through the National Retail Federation or similar trade associations.

Now you are ready to review the concepts that you have learned by using the spreadsheets for this chapter. Select the appropriate spreadsheets with which you have been working and answer the problems presented in **ASSIGNMENT 2.4**. Record your answers on the form provided.

FIGURE 2.5
Average Markup Percentage by Departments for Department Stores

Department	Year 1	Year 2
Female Apparel	53.1	53.3
Adult Female Accessories	54.9	55.0
Men's and Boy's Apparel and Accessories	52.7	53.7
Infant's and Children's Clothing and Accessories	52.3	53.0
Footwear	51.8	51.1

ASSIGNMENT 2.4

Chapter Review

The use of spreadsheets simplifies the calculations that buyers and merchandisers must make; however, they must know which spreadsheet to use for a specific calculation. Using the spreadsheets with which you have been working, fill in the blanks on the chart that follows.

	Unit Cost	Unit Retail	Markup Percentage
1.	$8.75		40%
2.	$8.99		45%
3.		$4.50	46.5%
4.	$8.99		43.5%
5.	$6.00	$11.75	
6.		$17.99	43.7%
7.	$16.80		41.4%
8.	$1.50		42%
9.	$18.66	$35.00	
10.	$21.78		39.9%
11.	$39.73	$79.95	
12.		$40.00	45.9%
13.	$6.00	$11.50	
14.	$12.60	$25.00	
15.	$40.23		46.3%

Chapter 3

Initial Markup

MERCHANDISING CONCEPT 3–1:
CALCULATE INITIAL MARKUP PERCENTAGES

To appropriately price merchandise, retailers must carefully plan their initial markup percentages. The *first* markup placed on merchandise is the ***initial markup***. In other words, initial markup is the difference between the cost of the merchandise and the *original* retail price. As illustrated in Figure 3.1, initial markup must cover a store's operating expenses and planned profit *as well as any reductions that may occur.* The initial markup percentage is based on estimated figures or predictions; therefore, inaccurate predictions will lead to inaccurate pricing decisions.

To plan the initial markup percentage, sales should be planned first. Usually, sales are planned based on past sales records as well as an examination of changes in internal and external conditions affecting the business. Expenses associated with this estimated sales level must be planned next. The amount of profit the retailer anticipates must then be estimated. Past store records or industry averages could be used to make this prediction. Finally, retailers must consider planned reductions that the store or department will experience.

Reductions include markdowns, discounts to employees and special groups of customers, and shortages. ***Markdowns*** occur any time the original retail price is lowered, and they are normally used to stimulate sales. At many stores, ***discounts*** are offered to employees as a fringe

FIGURE 3.1

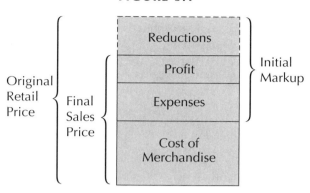

benefit of working there. Some retailers also give discounts to special groups of customers. For example, senior citizens may be given a discount on purchases they make on a specific day, or a paint store may offer discounts to painting contractors. **Shortages** can occur for a variety of reasons. Merchandise can be stolen by either employees or customers, and some shortages can be caused by paperwork errors such as employees improperly recording a sales transaction or making an error in counting merchandise for inventory purposes.

All these reductions must be considered when establishing the initial markup percentage. Reductions increase retail prices, so they must be controlled.

Two additional factors will also have an impact on the initial markup percentage that is planned. They are cash discounts and alteration/workroom expenses. These activities may not occur at all businesses. **Cash discounts** are given by manufacturers to retailers if they pay for merchandise on or before a stated discount date. For example, a retailer may be given terms such as "2/10, net 30," which means the retailer would receive a 2 percent discount if the bill is paid no later than 10 days after the date on the invoice; otherwise, the full amount must be paid within 30 days. Cash discounts reduce the cost of merchandise for the retailer; thus, initial markups can be lower, resulting in lower retail prices.

Alteration/workroom expenses occur when retailers make alterations or changes in their merchandise to satisfy special customer needs. Although most alteration/workroom expenses are associated with clothing sales, they may also occur when customers purchase items such as draperies, furniture, or jewelry. Alteration/workroom expenses are an extra expense of doing business, so they result in higher initial markups and, in the final analysis, higher retail prices.

Markups on merchandise usually do not stay the same during the course of a selling season. The price of merchandise that does not sell well is reduced. Some merchandise may be stolen or damaged, while in other cases discounts will be given to employees and customers. Rarely will the planned markup first placed on merchandise be realized when it is all finally sold.

The initial markup percentage can be calculated using the following formula:

Initial Markup % = (Expenses + Profit + Reductions + Alteration or Workroom Expenses − Cash Discounts)/(Sales + Reductions)

Buyers cannot use net sales alone as the base (or denominator) in the formula. The amount of retail reductions must be added to sales to obtain the correct amount of merchandise that initially needs to be purchased. Reductions include markdowns, employee discounts, and shortages.

SAMPLE PROBLEM

A store plans sales of $50,000 with a planned profit of $2,500. Reductions are estimated at $5,500. Expenses for this planned sales volume are estimated at $15,000. Using the preceding formula, calculate the initial markup percentage.

Sample Solution

Initial Markup = ($15,000 + $2,500 + $5,500)/($50,000 + $5,500)
Initial Markup = $23,000/$55,500
Initial Markup = .414
Initial Markup = 41.4%

The components of the initial markup formula can be estimated as either dollar amounts or as percentages. The markup percentage in this problem was calculated based on dollar amounts. However, most retailers plan initial markup using planned percentages of sales for each component in the formula. The assumption is that even though the dollar figures will change based on different sales estimates, each component's percentage of sales will remain fairly constant.

For example, expenses may be planned at 30 percent of sales, and a 5 percent profit is anticipated. Reductions are estimated at 11 percent of sales. Using the same formula, the initial markup percentage can be calculated using percentages rather than dollar figures. When using percent in the formula, sales will *always* equal 100 percent.

Initial Markup = (.30 + .05 + .11)/(1.00 + .11)
Initial Markup = .46/1.11
Initial Markup = .414
Initial Markup = 41.4%

Using Computerized Spreadsheets

Follow the instructions listed below to solve the sample problem that you just examined.

1. Place the *Merchandising CD* in drive D and load *Microsoft Excel*.
2. Select and open file **CH03-1-1** from drive D.
3. Using the numbers presented in the sample problem, input dollar amounts for each of the variables listed in the second column and percentages in the third column. Examine Figure 3.2 to check the accuracy of your input.
4. When you have completed your input, the initial markup percentage will have been calculated.
5. Use the spreadsheet to calculate the initial markup percentage for the problems that follow. Before entering any information in a cell, make sure that any previous entries have been erased. Record all your answers on the form for **ASSIGNMENT 3.1.1.**
6. When you have completed the lesson, **Save** the file under the file name **CH03-1-1A**, and then **Close** the file.
7. **Quit** the spreadsheet, unless you will be completing the next assignment immediately.

FIGURE 3.2

Calculating Initial Markup	Dollars	Percent
Expenses	$15,000.00	30.0%
Profit	$2,500.00	5.0%
Reductions	$5,500.00	11.0%
Sales	$50,000.00	100.0%
Initial Markup %		41.4%

Assignment Problems

1. Calculate the initial markup percentage for the following figures that have been estimated by the store owner:

Sales	$200,000
Expenses	$70,000
Reductions	$11,000
Profit	$14,000

2. A department manager wants to add a new classification of merchandise to the department. For this classification, expenses are anticipated to be 37 percent, and a profit of 6 percent is desired. Total reductions are estimated to be 8 percent. Calculate the initial markup percentage.

3. You have just been promoted to a buyer for children's clothing. One of your first duties is to plan the initial markup percentage for the department. Based on data from last year's reports, you expect reductions of 12 percent. Expenses are anticipated to be 29.9 percent. If a 9 percent profit is desired, calculate the initial markup percentage.

4. Calculate the initial markup percentage using the following data: expenses, $138,000; profits, $28,900; reductions, $21,200; and sales, $462,900.

5. Before opening a new department, store, management made the following estimates about its operations:

Reductions	$13,500
Sales	$316,500
Expenses	$105,000
Profit	$31,650

   Calculate the initial markup percentage.

ASSIGNMENT 3.1.1

Calculating Initial Markup Percentages

1.

Expenses	
Profit	
Reductions	
Sales	
Initial Markup Percentage	

2.

Expenses	
Profit	
Reductions	
Sales	
Initial Markup Percentage	

3.

Expenses	
Profit	
Reductions	
Sales	
Initial Markup Percentage	

4.

Expenses	
Profit	
Reductions	
Sales	
Initial Markup Percentage	

5.

Expenses	
Profit	
Reductions	
Sales	
Initial Markup Percentage	

Creating and Using Your Own Spreadsheet

The spreadsheet that you have been using does not incorporate several components of the initial markup percentage formula. Markdowns, employee/customer discounts, and shortages have not been listed separately. In addition, alteration/workroom expenses and cash discounts have not been used. You can design a spreadsheet that would allow you to calculate the initial markup percentage using *all* these components. Here is how it is done:

1. Using your *Merchandising CD*, follow instructions you have previously used to open file **CH03-1-2**. Type all your titles first. Press the **ENTER** key after typing each word. You will need to alter the width of column A. Your data will be entered into appropriate cells in column B.

RETAIL BUYING FIGURE 3.3

1	Expenses	
2	Profit	
3	Markdowns	
4	Discounts	
5	Shortages	
6	Alterations	
7	Cash Discounts	
8	Sales	
9	Initial Markup %	#DIV/0!

- In cell A1, type the word **Expenses.**
- In cell A2, type the word **Profit.**
- In cell A3, type the word **Markdowns.**
- In cell A4, type the word **Discounts.**
- In cell A5, type the word **Shortages.**
- In cell A6, type the word **Alterations.**
- In cell A7, type the words **Cash Discounts.**
- In cell A8, type the word **Sales.**
- In cell A9, type the words **Initial Markup %.**

2. Now, move to cell B15, and type the following formula after typing "=": **(B1 + B2 + B3 + B4 + B5 + B6 − B7)/(B8 + B3 + B4 + B5).** This formula programs the computer to calculate the initial markup percentage based on the formula that was presented earlier.
3. Use the **Format** command to display data to one decimal place.
4. When you have finished, your completed spreadsheet layout should resemble the one shown in Figure 3.3.
5. Complete the following problems using *your* spreadsheet. Record your answers on the form for **ASSIGNMENT 3.1.2**.
6. When you have completed the lesson, **Save** the file under the file name **CH03-1-2A**, and then **Close** the file.
7. **Quit** the spreadsheet, unless you will be completing the next assignment immediately.

Assignment Problems

1. John Amos is opening a women's ready-to-wear boutique. Sales have been estimated at $165,000. At that sales volume, expenses are expected

to be $59,000. Reductions are planned as follows: markdowns–$2,000, shortages–$1,500. No employee or customer discounts are allowed. Alteration/workroom expenses are estimated at $4,800. If John wants to earn $16,500 profit, what must the initial markup percentage be?

2. The owner of a small women's fashion store is adding a line of casual clothing. Based on industry averages for similar businesses, the following estimates have been made:

Expenses	37.3%
Cash Discounts	3.6%
Shortages	2.4%
Markdowns	7.6%
Employee Discounts	2.4%
Alteration Expenses	4.9%
Profits	7.2%

Using these estimates, calculate the initial markup percentage that is required.

3. Joanna Jones wants to expand her store to include a line of formal wear. She anticipates sales of $300,000 and a profit of $28,000. Based on the estimates listed below, calculate the initial markup percentage that would be required.

Expenses	$105,000
Employee Discounts	$2,900
Markdowns	$7,900
Workroom Expenses	$4,000
Shortages	$6,000
Cash Discounts	$11,500

4. The owner of a new business has the following estimates available: Expenses will run 35.4 percent with an anticipated profit of 8.5 percent. Workroom expenses are estimated at 1.7 percent, and cash discounts are expected to be 7.1 percent. Markdowns are planned at 3.4 percent, employee discounts are expected to be 1 percent, and shortages are predicted at 1.2 percent. Calculate the initial markup percentage.

5. Based on the following data, calculate the initial markup percentage.

Employee Discounts	$9,900
Profits	$46,700
Markdowns	$9,700
Expenses	$165,000
Sales	$583,000
Shortages	$7,000
Cash Discounts	$13,000

ASSIGNMENT 3.1.2					

Calculating Initial Markup Percentages

PROBLEM	1	2	3	4	5
Expenses					
Profit					
Markdowns					
Employee/ Customer Discounts					
Shortages					
Alteration/ Workroom Expenses					
Cash Discounts					
Sales					
Initial Markup Percentage					

MERCHANDISING CONCEPT 3–2: ESTIMATE SALES

The components that are used to calculate the initial markup percentage are all interrelated. Thus, the formula can also be used to estimate any *one* variable in the formula when all the other variables are either known or can be estimated.

Many times, retailers know the initial markup they must place on merchandise. They may have determined this information from past experience or by examining industry publications. If the initial markup percentage has been predetermined, retailers can use the formula you have been using to estimate the sales volume that would be required. The formula for initial markup percentage can be manipulated to make this calculation.

SAMPLE PROBLEM

A store owner is facing strong competition on prices and feels that initial markup must be lowered to 42.5 percent to match the competition. At that markup, the owner estimates expenses will not change and will remain at $35,000. The owner also expects reductions to decrease to

$12,000. Cash discounts are anticipated to remain at $3,000. Profits have been $16,000, and the owner wants to maintain them at that level. If the store owner prices merchandise with an initial markup of 42.5 percent and the other estimates are correct, what sales volume will be required?

Sample Solution

Simple algebra can be used to estimate the required sales volume. Substitute into the initial markup formula as shown, and then solve for the unknown variable–sales.

Initial Markup % = (Expenses + Profit + Reductions + Alteration or Workroom Expenses − Cash Discounts)/(Sales + Reductions)

$.425 = (35,000 + \$16,000 + \$12,000 − \$3,000)/(S + \$12,000)$

$.425 = \$60,000/(S + \$12,000)$

$.425 (S + \$12,000) = \$60,000$ (*multiply by S + \$12,000*)

$.425 S + \$5,100 = \$60,000$ (*multiply by .425*)

$.425 S = \$54,900$ (*divide both sides of equation by .425*)

Sales = $129,176.47

A sales volume of $129,176.47 would be required to generate a profit of $16,000 using a 42.5 percent initial markup. The store owner must examine past sales records as well as any changes that are expected in internal and external conditions to determine if this sales volume is an attainable goal.

Using Computerized Spreadsheets

Estimating sales volumes required at many different initial markup percentages can be quickly calculated using spreadsheets. Follow these instructions to solve the problems that follow.

1. Using your *Merchandising CD*, follow instructions you have previously used to open file **CH03-2**.
2. Using the numbers presented in the sample problem, input the correct amounts for each of the variables listed. Because a formula has already been entered, sales volume has been calculated.
3. Use the spreadsheet to estimate sales volume for the problems that follow. Record all your answers on the forms for **ASSIGNMENT 3.2**.
4. When you have completed the lesson, **Save** the file under the file name **CH03-2A**, and then **Close** the file.
5. **Quit** the spreadsheet, unless you will be completing the next assignment immediately.

Assignment Problems

1. You have just opened a new toy store and have obtained the following industry averages:

Expenses	$77,500
Profit	$15,000
Markdowns	$17,500
Employee Discounts	$7,500
Shortages	$3,750
Workroom Expenses	$1,250
Cash Discounts	$7,500
Initial Markup %	43.5%

   Calculate the estimated sales.

2. For the information presented in problem 1, examine the impact of raising the initial markup percentage to 45 percent. If all the other variables stay the same, estimate sales that would be required at this new initial markup.

3. Estimate sales for the information presented in problem 1 if you lowered the initial markup percentage to 41 percent.

4. After examining the retail prices of local competitors and studying his own expenses, the owner of a new men's clothing store has decided that a 45.8 percent initial markup will be needed for his business. The owner has consulted a local trade association and found the following figures to be average for similar stores in his area of the country:

Expenses	$29,000
Profit	$7,000
Markdowns	$13,000
Employee Discounts	$3,000
Shortages	$2,000
Alteration Expenses	$4,000
Cash Discounts	$4,000

   Calculate the required sales volume based on these estimates.

5. For the information presented in problem 4, estimate sales that would be required if the initial markup percentage were increased to 47.1 percent.

6. For the information presented in problem 4, estimate sales that would be required if the initial markup percentage were lowered to 44.1 percent.

ASSIGNMENT 3.2

Estimating Sales

1.

Initial Markup Percentage	
Expenses	
Profit	
Markdowns	
Employee/Customer Discounts	
Shortages	
Alteration/Workroom Costs	
Cash Discounts	
ESTIMATED SALES	

2.

Initial Markup Percentage	
Expenses	
Profit	
Markdowns	
Employee/Customer Discounts	
Shortages	
Alteration/Workroom Costs	
Cash Discounts	
ESTIMATED SALES	

3.

Initial Markup Percentage	
Expenses	
Profit	
Markdowns	
Employee/Customer Discounts	
Shortages	
Alteration/Workroom Costs	
Cash Discounts	
ESTIMATED SALES	

4.

Initial Markup Percentage	
Expenses	
Profit	
Markdowns	
Employee/Customer Discounts	
Shortages	
Alteration/Workroom Costs	
Cash Discounts	
ESTIMATED SALES	

5.

Initial Markup Percentage	
Expenses	
Profit	
Markdowns	
Employee/Customer Discounts	
Shortages	
Alteration/Workroom Costs	
Cash Discounts	
ESTIMATED SALES	

6.

Initial Markup Percentage	
Expenses	
Profit	
Markdowns	
Employee/Customer Discounts	
Shortages	
Alteration/Workroom Costs	
Cash Discounts	
ESTIMATED SALES	

MERCHANDISING CONCEPT 3–3: ESTIMATE PROFIT

Another type of analysis for which retailers regularly use the initial markup formula is estimating the operating profit that will result if the other variables are known or can be estimated. Retailers are interested in estimating the profit that would result at different sales levels when using different initial markups. Estimating profit can also be calculated using simple algebra with the initial markup formula.

SAMPLE PROBLEM

A buyer is facing strong competition on prices and feels that the initial markup must be lowered to 42.5 percent to match the competition. At that markup, the buyer estimates expenses will not change and will remain at approximately $35,000. Reductions are expected to decrease to $12,000. Cash discounts are anticipated to remain at $3,000. Sales have been $120,000, and the buyer estimates that lower prices will increase sales to $129,000. If the buyer prices merchandise with an initial markup of 42.5 percent and the other estimates are correct, what profit would result?

Sample Solution

Simple algebra can be used to estimate profit. Substitute into the initial markup formula as shown, and then solve for the unknown variable—profit.

Initial Markup % = (Expenses + Profit + Reductions + Alteration or
Workroom Expenses − Cash Discounts)/(Sales + Reductions)

$.425 = (\$35,000 + P + \$12,000 - \$3,000)/(\$129,000 + \$12,000)$

$.425 = (\$44,000 + P)/(\$141,000)$

$.425\ (\$141,000) = \$44,000 + P$ (*multiply by $141,000*)

$\$59,925 = \$44,000 + P$ (*multiply by .425*)

$P = \$15,925$ (*subtract $44,000*)

Estimated Profit = $15,925

An estimated profit of $15,925 would be generated with sales of $129,000 and a 42.5 percent initial markup. The buyer must examine past sales records as well as goals for the department to determine if this would be an acceptable level of profit.

Using Computerized Spreadsheets

Estimating profit at many different initial markup percentages and sales levels can be quickly calculated using spreadsheets. Follow these instructions to solve the problems that follow.

1. Using your *Merchandising CD*, follow instructions you have previously used to open file **CH03-3**.
2. Using the numbers presented in the sample problem, enter the correct amounts for each of the variables listed.
3. Use the spreadsheet to estimate profit for the problems that follow. Print your answers or record all your responses on the forms for **ASSIGNMENT 3.3**.

4. When you have completed the lesson, **Save** the file under the file name **CH03-3A** and then **Close** the file.

5. **Quit** the spreadsheet, unless you will be completing the next assignment immediately.

Assignment Problems

1. You have just opened a new toy store and have obtained the following industry averages:

Expenses	31%
Markdowns	7%
Employee Discounts	3%
Shortages	1.5%
Workroom Expenses	5%
Cash Discounts	3%
Initial Markup %	49.5%

After examining this information and the retail prices the competition is charging, you feel that an initial markup of 49.5 percent is too high. You believe that all the other estimates are realistic and attainable for your market. Calculate the estimated profit percentage if you decide to use a 45.9 percent initial markup.

2. You want to examine the impact of different initial markups on profit. For the information presented in problem 1, estimate profit using a 47 percent initial markup.

3. Estimate profit for the information presented in problem 1 if you lowered the initial markup to 41 percent.

4. After examining the retail prices of local competitors and studying his own expenses, the owner of a new men's clothing store has decided that a 45.8 percent initial markup will be needed for his business. The owner has consulted a local trade association and found the following figures to be average for similar stores in his area of the country:

Expenses	29%
Markdowns	13%
Employee Discounts	3%
Shortages	2%
Alteration Expenses	4%
Cash Discounts	4%

Estimate the profit percentage based on these figures.

5. For the information presented in problem 4, estimate the profit percentage if the initial markup were increased to 51.1 percent.
6. For the information presented in problem 4, estimate the profit percentage if the initial markup were lowered to 41.1 percent.

ASSIGNMENT 3.3

Estimating Profit

1.

Initial Markup Percentage	
Expenses	
Markdowns	
Employee/Customer Discounts	
Shortages	
Alteration/Workroom Costs	
Cash Discounts	
Sales	
ESTIMATED PROFIT	

2.

Initial Markup Percentage	
Expenses	
Markdowns	
Employee/Customer Discounts	
Shortages	
Alteration/Workroom Costs	
Cash Discounts	
Sales	
ESTIMATED PROFIT	

3.

Initial Markup Percentage	
Expenses	
Markdowns	
Employee/Customer Discounts	
Shortages	
Alteration/Workroom Costs	
Cash Discounts	
Sales	
ESTIMATED PROFIT	

4.

Initial Markup Percentage	
Expenses	
Markdowns	
Employee/Customer Discounts	
Shortages	
Alteration/Workroom Costs	
Cash Discounts	
Sales	
ESTIMATED PROFIT	

5.

Initial Markup Percentage	
Expenses	
Markdowns	
Employee/Customer Discounts	
Shortages	
Alteration/Workroom Costs	
Cash Discounts	
Sales	
ESTIMATED PROFIT	

6.

Initial Markup Percentage	
Expenses	
Markdowns	
Employee/Customer Discounts	
Shortages	
Alteration/Workroom Costs	
Cash Discounts	
Sales	
ESTIMATED PROFIT	

Chapter 4

Cumulative Markup

MERCHANDISING CONCEPT 4–1: CALCULATE CUMULATIVE MARKUP PERCENTAGE

As you have already learned, markup can be calculated for individual items; however, retailers more commonly report markups for a product category, a department, or an entire store for an extended period of time. In these situations, markup is referred to as cumulative markup. **Cumulative markup** is the markup achieved on all merchandise available for sale in a given period. Using cumulative markup is also more useful when comparing merchandising performance with established goals, past sales records, or with the performance of other stores.

A cumulative markup goal is often planned for a group of merchandise, but some individual items are usually given higher markups than this goal, while a lower markup is applied to other items. The cumulative markup is found by dividing the total markup in dollars (on all merchandise) by the total retail in dollars for all merchandise.

SAMPLE PROBLEM

At the start of a season, a buyer's inventory of scarves had the following values:

Total Cost	$3,000
Total Retail	$5,800

During the month, the following purchases were added to inventory:

> 50 scarves, costing $20 each, to retail at $40 each.
> 100 scarves, costing $10 each, to retail at $19 each.

What is the *cumulative markup percentage* to date?
Sample Solution

	Cost	Retail
Beginning Inventory	$3,000	$5,800
Purchases	$1,000 (50 × $20)	$2,000 (50 × $40)
Purchases	$1,000 (100 × $10)	$1,900 (100 × $19)
Totals	$5,000	$9,700

Next, calculate total markup in dollars by subtracting total cost from total retail:

$$\$9,700 - \$5,000 = \$4,700$$

Finally, calculate cumulative markup percentage by dividing total markup in dollars by total retail:

$$\$4,700/\$9,700 = 48.5\%$$

The cumulative markup percentage is 48.5 percent.

Using Computerized Spreadsheets

Finding cumulative markup is a mathematical calculation that buyers and merchandisers may need to know after every purchase has arrived in the store and been placed on the sales floor. Using a computerized spreadsheet allows them to perform this activity quickly. Follow the instructions listed below to solve the sample problem that you just examined.

1. Using your *Merchandising CD*, follow instructions you have previously used to open file **CH04-1-1**.
2. Use the numbers presented in the sample problem to enter the beginning inventory and purchases at cost and retail.
3. Because a formula has already been entered, the computer has calculated total cost, total retail, and the cumulative markup percentage. You can now determine cumulative markup percentage by using this spread-

sheet for any situation involving a beginning inventory and one or two purchases.

4. Use the spreadsheet to calculate the cumulative markup percent for the problems that follow.

5. **Print** the answers to each problem or record all your answers on the forms for **ASSIGNMENT 4.1.1**.

6. When you have completed the lesson, **Save** the file under the file name **CH04-1-1A**, and then **Close** the file.

7. **Quit** the spreadsheet, unless you will be completing the next assignment immediately.

Assignment Problems

1. The buyer of scarves in the sample problem wants to calculate the cumulative markup percentage at the time the first purchases were added to beginning inventory. Calculate the cumulative markup percentage at that point.

2. Beginning inventory was $58,932 at cost and $106,342 at retail. Purchases for the period were $13,467 at cost and $24,916 at retail. What was the cumulative markup percentage for the period?

3. A specialty store had a beginning inventory at cost of $161,358. At retail, the inventory was valued at $261,400. Two purchases were added to inventory. At cost, they had a value of $82,700 and $244,058, respectively. At retail, purchase 1 was valued at $137,282 and purchase 2 was valued at $398,682. What was the cumulative markup percentage for the period?

4. A buyer for sporting goods has an inventory at the beginning of the month of $30,000 at cost and $45,000 at retail. New purchases during the month amounted to $20,000 at cost and $35,000 at retail. What is the cumulative markup percentage?

ASSIGNMENT 4.1.1

Calculating Cumulative Markup Percentages

1.

	Cost	Retail	Markup Percentage
Beginning Inventory			
Purchases			
Totals			

2.

	Cost	Retail	Markup Percentage
Beginning Inventory			
Purchases			
Totals			

3.

	Cost	Retail	Markup Percentage
Beginning Inventory			
Purchases 1			
Purchases 2			
Totals			

4.

	Cost	Retail	Markup Percentage
Beginning Inventory			
Purchases			
Totals			

Creating and Using Your Own Spreadsheet

The spreadsheet that you have been using can be used only if you have two or fewer purchases added to beginning inventory. However, you can design a spreadsheet that would allow you to calculate cumulative markup percentage for any number of purchases that you desire. Here is how it is done for a retailer who adds purchases to inventory once a week and wants to calculate cumulative markup percentage.

1. Using your *Merchandising CD*, follow instructions you have previously used to open file **CH04-1-2**. Type all your titles first. Press **ENTER** after typing each word.
   - In cell B2, type the word **Cost.**
   - In cell C2, type the word **Retail.**
   - In cell D2, type the word **Markup %.**
   - In cell A3, type the words **Beginning Inventory.**
   - In cell A4, type the word **Purchases 1.**
   - In cell A5, type the word **Purchases 2.**
   - In cell A6, type the word **Purchases 3.**
   - In cell A7, type the word **Purchases 4.**
   - In cell A8, type the word **Totals.**
   - In cell B8, after typing "=", type **SUM (B3:B7).** This programs the computer to add all numbers in cells B3, B4, B5, B6, and B7.

FIGURE 4.1

Cumulative Markup			
	Cost	Retail	Markup %
Beginning Inventory			
Purchases 1			
Purchases 2			
Purchases 3			
Purchases 4			
TOTALS	$0.00	$0.00	#DIV/0!

- In cell C8, after typing "=", type **SUM (C3:C7)**. This programs the computer to add all numbers in cells C3, C4, C5, C6, and C7.
- In cell D8, after typing "=", type **(C8 − B8)/C8**. This programs the computer to subtract total cost from total retail and then divide the resulting number by total retail, providing you with the cumulative markup percentage.

2. When you have finished, your completed spreadsheet screen should resemble the one shown in Figure 4.1.
3. Use the spreadsheet you have designed to complete the problems that follow. Record all your answers on the forms for **ASSIGNMENT 4.1.2**.
4. When you have completed the lesson, **Save** the file under the file name **CH04-1-2A**, and then **Close** the file.
5. **Quit** the spreadsheet, unless you will be completing the next assignment immediately.

Assignment Problems

1. A buyer at a local specialty store had beginning inventory at cost of $50,000. At retail its value was $97,678. During the month of May purchases were added to inventory on a weekly basis in the following manner:

	Cost	Retail
Week 1	$3,770	$6,500
Week 2	$9,100	$14,000
Week 3	$8,000	$12,500
Week 4	$4,640	$8,000

Calculate the cumulative markup percentage at the end of the first week.

2. Calculate the cumulative markup percentage at the end of the second week.
3. Calculate the cumulative markup percentage at the end of the third week.
4. Calculate the cumulative markup percentage at the end of the fourth week.

ASSIGNMENT 4.1.2

Calculating Cumulative Markup Percentages

1.

	Cost	Retail	Markup Percentage
Beginning Inventory			
Purchases			
Totals			

2.

	Cost	Retail	Markup Percentage
Beginning Inventory			
Purchases 1			
Purchases 2			
Totals			

3.

	Cost	Retail	Markup Percentage
Beginning Inventory			
Purchases 1			
Purchases 2			
Purchases 3			
Totals			

4.

	Cost	Retail	Markup Percentage
Beginning Inventory			
Purchases 1			
Purchases 2			
Purchases 3			
Purchases 4			
Totals			

MERCHANDISING CONCEPT 4–2: CALCULATE MARKUP PERCENTAGE NEEDED ON NEW PURCHASES

Buyers must plan cumulative markup goals for their store or departments. Typically, the cumulative markup percentage on all merchandise in a department is one of the most critical goals for the buyer to plan and establish. To effectively reach this goal, merchandise must be purchased and priced in such a way that, at the end of the season, the cumulative markup goal will be achieved.

By defining their goals, buyers give themselves a way to measure their performance. In addition, buyers must change their strategies when goals are not being met. By *periodically* measuring their progress toward reaching their cumulative markup goal, buyers can make changes in their merchandising strategy before the end of the selling season when it would be too late to achieve their goal.

Pricing merchandise would be simple if the same markup were applied to all items that are purchased during a season; however, this seldom occurs. Some items will carry higher or lower markups for a variety of reasons. Some items carry a higher markup because there is a greater risk of theft. Fashion merchandise is usually given a higher markup than basic items. Demand for some fashion items changes quickly, and a product that sells quickly today may be tomorrow's big markdown. Also, when an item is first introduced, a lower markup may be used to build store traffic. Later retail prices on the item would probably reflect a higher markup. Other factors may also affect the markup that is used during the season. Wholesale prices may have been increased by a manufacturer in the middle of the season, or some retail prices may have been reduced during the season to meet competitors' prices. In Figure 4.2, median and superior cumulative markup percentages from past years can be found for some selected departments within department stores.

As a season progresses, buyers must track cumulative markup on their purchases. Any of the occurrences described earlier could result in different markups for merchandise in a department; therefore, in order to achieve the planned cumulative markup percentage, different markups will have to be used on the balance of purchases made during the season. For example, if the cumulative markup to date is slipping below the departmental goal, higher markups will be required on future purchases. Buyers must be able to estimate what this new markup should be to realize the planned cumulative markup for the season. Buyers can easily make that estimate using some of the basic concepts you have already learned.

FIGURE 4.2
Cumulative Markup Percentages
Department Stores

	Median	Superior
Fine Jewelry and Watches	52.6	54.6
Costume Jewelry	56.2	58.3
Hosiery	52.4	54.2
Gloves	55.6	56.7
Handbags	55.2	57.0
Small Leather Goods	55.5	57.5

When making new purchases, buyers must keep in mind their cumulative markup goal and how to achieve it. Anytime during the season, buyers can calculate their cumulative markup. They must subtract purchases already made from total planned purchases. The difference or balance represents the amount remaining to be spent. Using this basic concept in the problem that follows, you can calculate the markup percentage needed on the balance of the purchases.

SAMPLE PROBLEM

A buyer plans to purchase $40,000 (at retail) worth of shirts for the spring season. A cumulative markup of 48 percent is desired. Early in the season, $18,000 was spent on shirts. The total retail of this purchase was $36,000. Now, the buyer must determine the markup percentage that must be obtained on the balance of the purchases to achieve the cumulative markup.

Sample Solution

The calculation can be made using the following steps:

Step One. Record the information that has occurred.

	Cost	Retail	Markup %
Total Planned Purchases		$40,000	48%
Purchases Already Made	$18,000	$36,000	
Balance	_____	_____	_____

Step Two. Determine the cost of planned purchases.

Cost = Retail × (100% − Markup %)
Cost = $40,000 × .52
Cost = $20,800

Step Three. Next, calculate both the cost and retail values of the balance of the purchases.

Cost of Total Planned Purchases	$20,800
− Cost of Purchases Already Made	$18,000
= Cost of Balance of Purchases	$2,800

Retail of Total Planned Purchases	$40,000
− Retail of Purchases Already Made	$36,000
= Retail of Balance of Purchases	$4,000

Step Four. Calculate the markup percentage for the balance of the purchases.

Markup % = Markup in Dollars/Total Retail
Markup % = ($4,000 − $2,800)/$4,000
Markup % = 30%

Therefore, only a 30-percent markup could be placed on all remaining purchases for the season, and the desired 48 percent cumulative markup percentage could still be achieved.

Using Computerized Spreadsheets

Calculating the markup percentage needed on remaining purchases for a season can be calculated after every purchase has been made. Using a computerized spreadsheet allows buyers to perform this activity very quickly. Follow the instructions listed below to solve the sample problem that you just examined:

1. Using your *Merchandising CD*, follow instructions you have previously used to open file **CH04-2**.

FIGURE 4.3

Cumulative Markup			
	Cost	Retail	Markup Percentage
Planned Purchases	$20,800.00	$40,000.00	0.480
Already Purchased	$18,000.00	$36,000.00	
Balance of Purchase	$2,800.00	$4,000.00	0.300

2. Using the numbers presented in the sample problem, enter the planned retail purchases for the season and the desired markup. Then enter the purchases to date at cost and retail.
3. The computer calculates the balance of purchases at cost and retail as well as the markup that will be needed on these remaining purchases. Examine Figure 4.3 to check the accuracy of your input.
4. You can now determine the markup percentage needed on remaining purchases by using this spreadsheet. Use this spreadsheet to calculate the markup percentage for the problems that follow. Record all your answers on the forms for **ASSIGNMENT 4.2**.
5. When you have completed the lesson, **Save** the file under the file name **CH04-2A** and then **Close** the file.
6. **Quit** the spreadsheet, unless you will be completing the next assignment immediately.

Assignment Problems

1. A sportswear buyer has plans to purchase raincoats for the season and retail them for $3,000 ($15 each). To date, the buyer has purchased $1,530 worth of raincoats that have been retailed for $2,550. What markup percentage must be used on the balance of the purchases if the planned cumulative markup for raincoats is 42 percent?
2. Jake Thomas has already spent $35,340 for merchandise to sell for $62,000. The season's plan is for purchases totaling $95,000 at retail with a 42 percent cumulative markup percentage. What markup percentage can Jake place on the balance of the purchases and still achieve the cumulative markup goal?

3. The buyer for men's clothing has projected that $280,000 (at retail) worth of merchandise will be needed for the season. The planned cumulative markup percentage goal is 49.5. Already in inventory at the start of the season is merchandise that has a total cost of $88,000 and a total retail value of $168,000. What markup percentage must the buyer obtain on the remaining purchases to achieve the cumulative markup goal?

4. A buyer plans to spend $50,000 at retail for the spring sale and wants to achieve a 51.4 percent cumulative markup percentage. From one vendor, the buyer purchases merchandise for $1,100 that will retail for $2,000. What markup percentage must be achieved on the balance of the purchases to achieve the desired cumulative markup?

5. A buyer for accessories plans to purchase merchandise that will retail for $11,000. The buyer's markup goal is 46.5 percent. To date, purchases have amounted to $4,480 at cost and $8,000 at retail. What must the markup percentage be on the remaining purchases to achieve the markup goal?

ASSIGNMENT 4.2

Calculating Markup Percentages for New Purchases

1.

	Cost	Retail	Markup Percentage
Planned Purchases			
Already Purchased			
Balance of Purchases			

2.

	Cost	Retail	Markup Percentage
Planned Purchases			
Already Purchased			
Balance of Purchases			

3.

	Cost	Retail	Markup Percentage
Planned Purchases			
Already Purchased			
Balance of Purchases			

4.

	Cost	Retail	Markup Percentage
Planned Purchases			
Already Purchased			
Balance of Purchases			

5.

	Cost	Retail	Markup Percentage
Planned Purchases			
Already Purchased			
Balance of Purchases			

Chapter 5

Markdowns and Markdown Cancellations

MERCHANDISING CONCEPT 5–1:
CALCULATE TOTAL DOLLAR MARKDOWNS

The same markup is usually not achieved on all items within a product category during a selling season. Many times, the retail prices of items sold near the end of the season have to be reduced. In other words, a markdown has occurred. Because markdowns reduce the planned markup, anticipated profits are also reduced; therefore, markdowns must be carefully controlled. Athough markdowns reduce profits, they are a fact of life in retailing. Moreover, most retailers use markdowns as a promotional tool–to draw customers into the store and increase store traffic.

Accurately planning and controlling markdowns is crucial to the profitability of a retail business. Markdowns have a significant impact on the sales revenue that a store generates. If markdowns are estimated at too high a level, the initial markup will also be high, which may cause retail prices to be much higher than those of the competition. Conversely, if markdowns are estimated at too low a level, the resulting initial markup may not be high enough to provide sufficient gross margin to produce a satisfactory profit. *Gross margin* is the sales revenue that remains after cost of goods sold has been deducted. In order for a business to earn a profit, gross margin must be more than expenses.

A markdown can be expressed as a dollar amount or as a percentage of net sales and is usually planned for an entire season just as buyers plan initial markup percentage, sales, purchases, expenses, and profits.

A markdown (expressed in dollars) is simply the difference between the original retail price of an item and its current retail price after price reductions have been made. Rather than being concerned with the markdown on *one* item, most buyers calculate markdowns for an entire group of items. To calculate total markdown in dollars, the dollar markdown on one item is multiplied by the number of units that are marked down.

SAMPLE PROBLEM

Based on the following information, a buyer wants to determine the total dollar markdown for a department in which the prices of the following two items were reduced.

Stock #	Items in Stock	Original Retail	Sale Price
1435	210	$24.99	$19.99
5684	55	$5.69	$5.00

Sample Solution

First, determine the markdown on each individual item. Then multiply that markdown by the number of items in stock. Because more than one type of merchandise is being reduced, add the totals.

For Stock # 1435	($24.99 − $19.99) × 210 = $1,050.00
For Stock # 5684	($5.69 − $5.00) × 55 = $37.95
Total Markdowns Taken	$1,050.00 + $37.95 = $1,087.95

Using Computerized Spreadsheets

Markdowns are a relatively simple operation for retailers who have computerized their entire operation. However, many small retailers still make many of their calculations with only a personal computer or calculator. Using a spreadsheet can greatly speed up the calculation of total markdowns in these situations.

1. Using your *Merchandising CD*, follow instructions you have previously used to open file **CH05-1**.
2. Enter the data used in the sample problem to solve that problem.

FIGURE 5.1

Markdowns				
	# in Stock	Original Retail	Sale Price	Markdown $
Stock #	210	$24.99	$19.99	$1,050.00
Stock #	55	$5.69	$5.00	$37.95
Stock #				$0.00
Stock #				$0.00
TOTAL MARKDOWNS				$1,087.95

3. Examine Figure 5.1 to check the accuracy of your input. Then, calculate the total markdown in dollars for the problems that follow. Record all your answers on the forms for **ASSIGNMENT 5.1**.
4. When you have completed the lesson, **Save** the file under the file name **CH05-1A**, and then **Close** the file.
5. **Quit** the spreadsheet, unless you will be completing the next assignment immediately.

Assignment Problems

1. For a monthly promotion, four items were marked down. In the table below, original and sale prices are given as well as the number of items in stock. Calculate the total markdown in dollars.

Stock #	Items in Stock	Original Retail	Sale Price
9865	1,870	$14.99	$11.99
6684	155	$15.69	$13.00
7778	34	$59.99	$49.99
9976	1,987	$9.99	$7.50

2. In preparation for a sale, all brands of men's shirts were reduced 20 percent. Calculate the total markdown in dollars for men's shirts.

Stock #	Items in Stock	Original Retail	Sale Price
1234	50	$24.99	$19.99
1235	55	$19.99	$15.99
1236	35	$34.99	$27.99

3. Calculate the total markdown in dollars for the following items:

Stock #	Items in Stock	Original Retail	Sale Price
9435	1,210	$4.99	$3.75
7684	455	$6.69	$5.00
8787	590	$8.29	$6.25
9876	621	$7.99	$5.99

4. Calculate the total markdown in dollars for the following items:

Stock #	Items in Stock	Original Retail	Sale Price
2435	36	$49.00	$39.00
2684	27	$35.00	$27.00
2787	48	$29.00	$21.00
2876	60	$19.00	$15.00

ASSIGNMENT 5.1

Calculating Total Dollar Markdowns

1.

# in Stock	Original Retail	Sale Price	Markdown $
Total Markdown in Dollars			

2.

# in Stock	Original Retail	Sale Price	Markdown $
Total Markdown in Dollars			

3.

# in Stock	Original Retail	Sale Price	Markdown $
Total Markdown in Dollars			

4.

# in Stock	Original Retail	Sale Price	Markdown $
Total Markdown in Dollars			

MERCHANDISING CONCEPT 5–2: CALCULATE MARKDOWN PERCENTAGE

Most retailers find that it is more useful to express markdowns as a percentage of net sales rather than in dollars. Showing markdowns as a percentage allows them to make comparisons among different departments. Percentages also allow retailers to easily compare the markdowns for a store or a department with industry averages such as those shown in Figure 5.2.

The formula for calculating markdown percentage is as follows:

Markdown Percentage = Total $ Markdown/$ Net Sales

Total dollar markdown is found by subtracting the final selling price of an item from its original retail price and then multiplying by the number of items in stock.

FIGURE 5.2
Average Markdown Percentages for Selected Departments

Department	
Female Apparel	35.2
Adult Female Accessories	18.2
Men's and Boy's Apparel and Accessories	27.9
Infant's and Children's Clothing and Accessories	30.0
Footwear	26.8
Cosmetics and Drugs	1.7
Home Furnishings	21.2
Leisure and Home Electronics	19.7

SAMPLE PROBLEM

Based on the following information, a buyer wants to determine the markdown percentage for a department in which the prices of only two items were reduced. Net sales for the department were $60,445.

The prices of these two items were reduced as follows:

Stock #	Items in Stock	Original Retail	Sale Price
1435	210	$24.99	$19.99
5684	55	$5.69	$5.00

Sample Solution:
First, determine the markdown on each individual item. Then multiply that markdown by the number of items in stock. Because more than one type of merchandise is being reduced, add the totals.

For Stock # 1435 ($24.99 − $19.99) × 210 = $1,050.00
For Stock # 5684 ($5.69 − $5.00) × 55 = $37.95
Total Markdowns Taken $1,050.00 + $37.95 = $1,087.95

Next, determine the markdown percentage by dividing total markdowns in dollars by net sales.

Markdown Percentage = Total $ Markdown/$ Net Sales
Markdown Percentage = $1,087.95/$60,445.00
Markdown Percentage = .01799
Markdown Percentage = 1.8%

Buyers can evaluate their performance by comparing their markdown percentages with stated goals, similar departments, or industry averages. If the markdown percentage is higher, changes in strategy must be planned.

Using Computerized Spreadsheets

1. Using your *Merchandising CD*, follow instructions you have previously used to open file **CH05-2-1**.
2. Enter the data used in the sample problem to solve that problem. Then, calculate the total markdown percentage for the problems that follow. Record all your answers on the forms for **ASSIGNMENT 5.2.1**.

3. When you have completed the lesson, **Save** the file under the file name **CH05-2-1A**, and then **Close** the file.
4. **Quit** the spreadsheet, unless you will be completing the next assignment immediately.

Assignment Problems

1. Sports shirts selling for $24.99 were reduced by $5.00. What was the markdown percentage on one shirt?
2. A shoe department had total sales of $65,000. Markdowns for the period amounted to $3,450. Calculate the markdown percentage.
3. Markdowns in Department A amounted to $7,678 for the month. Monthly departmental sales totaled $219,937. What was the markdown percentage for Department A?
4. Seasonal markdowns for a small toy store amounted to $8,900. Sales for the period were $279,678.29. Calculate the store's markdown percentage.
5. A department had seasonal sales of $329,762. Dollar markdowns for specific classifications are presented below. For each classification, calculate the markdown percentage.

Classification	$ Markdowns
45687	$589
45688	$1,908
45689	$451
45690	$59

ASSIGNMENT 5.2.1

Calculating Dollar Markdowns and Markdown Percentages

1.

Sales	
$ Markdowns	
Markdown %	

2.

Sales	
$ Markdowns	
Markdown %	

3.

Sales	
$ Markdowns	
Markdown %	

4.

Sales	
$ Markdowns	
Markdown %	

5.

Classification	$ Markdowns	Markdown %

Creating and Using Your Own Spreadsheet

You can design a spreadsheet that will allow you to compute total dollar markdowns as well as markdown percentages.

1. Using your *Merchandising CD*, follow instructions you have previously used to open file **CH05-2-2**. Beginning in cell B3, type the titles that follow as headings of individual columns. You will probably want to abbreviate most of them. Your completed spreadsheet layout should resemble the one shown in Figure 5.3.
   - **Stock Number**
   - **Original Unit Retail**
   - **Unit Sale Price**
   - **Dollar Markdowns**
   - **Markdown % of Total Sales**

FIGURE 5.3

Markdown Percentages						
Total Dollar Sales	$0.00					
	Stock #	Org. Unit Retail	Unit Sale Price	# in Stock	Dollar Markdowns	Markdown %

2. Because all the problems with which you will be working involve three different classification/stock numbers, you will need to set up your formulas three times to calculate dollar markdowns for each item.
   • In the cell below the heading "Dollar Markdowns," type a formula that will (1) calculate the difference between the original retail price and the sale price for the classification of merchandise in that row, and (2) multiply that difference by the number of items of that classification in inventory.
   • In the second cell below "Dollar Markdowns," type a formula that will perform a similar mathematical calculation for the classification of merchandise in that row.
   • Repeat this procedure for the third row.
3. Now you need to calculate the markdown percentage that each classification represents of total sales.
   • In the cell below the column heading "Markdown Percentage," type a formula that will calculate the percentage that "Dollar Markdowns" represents of "Total Dollar Sales."
   • Type in formulas that will perform similar calculations for merchandise classifications in the second and third rows below the "Markdown Percentage" heading.
4. Use the spreadsheet to answer the questions that follow. Record all your answers on the forms for **ASSIGNMENT 5.2.2**.
5. When you have completed the lesson, **Save** the file under the file name **CH05-2-2A**, and then **Close** the file.
6. **Quit** the spreadsheet, unless you will be completing the next assignment immediately.

Assignment Problems

1. Monthly departmental sales were $98,765. Permanent markdowns were taken on the following items in the amounts listed. Calculate the markdown percentage for each item separately.

Stock #	Original Retail	Sale Price	# in Inventory
1234	$29.99	$25.00	38
1235	$39.99	$35.00	46
1236	$59.99	$50.00	28

2. At the beginning of the month, men's short-sleeve Gant shirts were reduced from $29.99 to $25.00. At the same time, Arrow shirts were reduced from $24.99 to $19.99. Fifty-four Gant shirts and 70 Arrow shirts were in stock when the markdowns were made. At the end of the month,

total sales for men's shirts amounted to $55,211. Calculate the markdown percentage for each shirt.

3. Monthly departmental sales were $198,465. Permanent markdowns were taken on the following items in the amounts listed. Calculate the markdown percentage for each item separately.

Stock #	Original Retail	Sale Price	# in Inventory
1234	$79.99	$65.00	28
1235	$59.99	$45.00	56
1236	$99.99	$80.00	38

ASSIGNMENT 5.2.2
Calculating Dollar Markdowns and Markdown Percentages

1.

Stock	Original Retail	Sale Price	Number in Stock	$ Markdown	Markdown %

2.

Stock	Original Retail	Sale Price	Number in Stock	$ Markdown	Markdown %

3.

Stock	Original Retail	Sale Price	Number in Stock	$ Markdown	Markdown %

MERCHANDISING CONCEPT 5–3:
CALCULATE OFF-RETAIL PERCENTAGE

For internal control purposes within a retail store, markdowns are always expressed as a percentage of net sales. Customers, however, are more interested in a markdown off the original retail price. This percentage is referred to as the *off-retail percentage* and is used extensively in retail advertising.

To calculate off-retail percentages, the dollar markdown for an item is divided by the original retail price of the item, not the final sales price. This calculation is expressed in the following formula:

Off-Retail % = Dollar Markdown/Original Retail Price

SAMPLE PROBLEM

An item is reduced from $100 to $75. What is the off-retail percentage?

Sample Solution

Off-Retail % = Dollar Markdown/Original Retail Price
Off-Retail % = ($100 − $75)/$100
Off-Retail % = $25/$100
Off-Retail % = .25 or 25%

Using Computerized Spreadsheets

1. Select and open file **CH05-3**.
2. Enter the data used in the illustrative problem to solve that problem. Then, calculate the off-retail percentage for the problems that follow. Record all your answers on the forms for **ASSIGNMENT 5.3**.
3. When you have completed the lesson, **Save** the file under the file name **CH05-3A**, and then **Close** the file.
4. **Quit** the spreadsheet, unless you will be completing the next assignment immediately.

Assignment Problems

1. An item was reduced from $75 to $50. What off-retail percentage could be advertised?
2. Blouses were reduced from $27.50 to $20.00. What off-retail percentage can be advertised?
3. VCRs were reduced from $248.99 to $186.00. What off-retail percentage can be advertised?

4. All the items listed below were reduced for an end-of-season sale. What off-retail percentage could be advertised for each one?

Stock #	Original Retail	Sale Price
3456	$59.99	$47.99
3457	$49.99	$39.99
3458	$39.99	$29.99
3459	$29.99	$20.00
3460	$19.99	$15.99

ASSIGNMENT 5.3

Calculating Off-Retail Percentages

1.

Original Retail	
Sale Price	
Off-Retail Percentage	

2.

Original Retail	
Sale Price	
Off-Retail Percentage	

3.

Original Retail	
Sale Price	
Off-Retail Percentage	

4.

Stock #	Original Retail	Sale Price	Off-Retail %

MERCHANDISING CONCEPT 5–4: CALCULATE MARKDOWN CANCELLATIONS

For many promotions involving markdowns early in the selling season, all the items in stock that were marked down probably will not sell at the reduced price. For example, a promotion such as a Washington's Birthday sale may last for only a few days. At the end of the sale, merchandise is repriced, usually at the original retail price. A *markdown cancellation* has occurred. Retailers must track and control these cancellations because they have an impact on the value of inventory at retail.

SAMPLE PROBLEM

One hundred items that had an original retail price of $12 each were marked down $2 each for a special sale. Ninety of the items sold at the sale price, and the others were repriced at $12 when the sale was over. What was the dollar amount of the markdown cancellation?

Sample Solution

A $20 markdown cancellation would be recorded for this item ($2 price increase × 10 remaining in stock).

Using Computerized Spreadsheets

1. Using your *Merchandising CD*, follow instructions you have previously used to open file **CH05-4-1**.
2. Use the spreadsheet to complete the problems that follow. Record all your answers on the forms for **ASSIGNMENT 5.4.1**.
3. When you have completed the lesson, **Save** the file under the file name **CH05-41–A**, and then **Close** the file.
4. **Quit** the spreadsheet, unless you will be completing the next assignment immediately.

Assignment Problems

1. The prices of the following items were reduced for a three-day sale. At the end of the sale, prices were returned to the original retail price. Calculate the total markdown cancellation.

Original Retail	Sale Price	On Hand	Sold
$3.99	$2.99	42	36
$5.99	$4.99	35	29
$6.99	$5.99	29	26

2. The prices of the following items were reduced for a Labor Day weekend sale. At the end of the sale, prices were returned to the original retail price. Calculate the total markdown cancellation.

Original Retail	Sale Price	On Hand	Sold
$5.99	$5.00	116	101
$5.59	$4.75	124	75
$4.59	$4.00	126	100

3. The prices of the following two items were reduced for a one-day sale. At the end of the sale, prices were returned to the original retail price. Calculate the total markdown cancellation.

Original Retail	Sale Price	On Hand	Sold
$49.00	$39.00	36	15
$35.00	$27.00	36	18

4. The prices of the following items were reduced for a three-day sale. At the end of the sale, prices were returned to the original retail price. Calculate the total markdown cancellation.

Original Retail	Sale Price	On Hand	Sold
$13.99	$10.99	150	96
$24.59	$15.99	72	48
$11.99	$7.99	145	115
$32.99	$25.00	95	55

ASSIGNMENT 5.4.1

Calculating Markdown Cancellations

1.

Original Retail	Sale Price	On Hand	Sold	$ Cancellation
Total Markdown Cancellation				

2.

Original Retail	Sale Price	On Hand	Sold	$ Cancellation
Total Markdown Cancellation				

3.

Original Retail	Sale Price	On Hand	Sold	$ Cancellation
Total Markdown Cancellation				

4.

Original Retail	Sale Price	On Hand	Sold	$ Cancellation
Total Markdown Cancellation				

Creating and Using Your Own Spreadsheet

You can design a spreadsheet that will allow you to compute total dollar markdowns as well as markdown cancellations.

1. Using your *Merchandising CD,* follow instructions you have previously used to open file **CH05-4-2**. Type the titles that follow as headings of individual columns. You will probably want to abbreviate most of them. Your completed spreadsheet screen should resemble the one shown in Figure 5.4.
   - **Classification/Stock Number**
   - **Original Unit Retail Price**

FIGURE 5.4

Classification	Org. Retail	Sale Price	On Hand	# Sold	$ M/D	M/D Cancellations
					$0.00	$0.00
					$0.00	$0.00
					$0.00	$0.00
					$0.00	$0.00

- **Unit Sale Price**
- **Number in Inventory (On Hand)**
- **Number Sold**
- **Dollar Markdowns**
- **Markdown Cancellations**

2. Because all the problems with which you will be working involve three different classification/stock numbers, you will need to set up your formulas three times to calculate dollar markdowns and markdown cancellations for each item. Remember to press the "=" sign before entering your formulas.

- In the cell below the heading "Dollar Markdowns," enter a formula that will (a) calculate the difference between the original retail price and the sale price for the classification of merchandise on that row, and (b) multiply that difference by the number of items sold.
- In the second cell below "Dollar Markdowns," type a formula that will perform a similar mathematical calculation for the classification of merchandise on that row.
- Repeat this procedure for the third row.
- Now you need to calculate the markdown cancellation for each classification. In the cell below the column heading "Markdown Cancellation," enter a formula that will (a) calculate the difference between the new retail price and the sale price for the classification of merchandise on that row, and (b) multiply that difference by the number of items *not* sold.

3. Use your spreadsheet to complete the problems that follow. Record all your answers on the forms for **ASSIGNMENT 5.4.2**.

4. When you have completed the lesson, **Save** the file under the file name **CH05-4-2A**, and then **Close** the file.

5. **Quit** the spreadsheet, unless you will be completing the next assignment immediately.

Assignment Problems

1. The prices of the following items were reduced for a three-day sale. At the end of the sale, prices were returned to the original retail price. Calculate the dollar markdown and the markdown cancellation for each item.

Classification	Original Retail	Sale Price	On Hand	Sold
12345	$3.99	$2.99	42	36
12346	$5.99	$4.99	35	29
12347	$6.99	$5.99	29	26

2. The prices of the following items were reduced for a Labor Day weekend sale. At the end of the sale, prices were returned to the original retail price. Calculate the dollar markdown and markdown cancellations for each item.

Classification	Original Retail	Sale Price	On Hand	Sold
12654	$5.99	$5.00	116	101
12653	$5.59	$4.75	124	75
12652	$4.59	$4.00	126	100

3. The prices of the following two items were reduced for a one-day sale. At the end of the sale, prices were returned to the original retail price. Calculate the dollar markdowns and markdown cancellations for each item.

Classification	Original Retail	Sale Price	On Hand	Sold
98987	$49.00	$39.00	36	15
98986	$35.00	$27.00	36	18

4. The prices of the following items were reduced for a three-day sale. At the end of the sale, prices were returned to the original retail price. Calculate the dollar markdowns and markdown cancellations for each item.

Classification	Original Retail	Sale Price	On Hand	Sold
67678	$13.99	$10.99	150	96
67679	$24.59	$15.99	72	48
67670	$11.99	$7.99	145	115

ASSIGNMENT 5.4.2
Calculating Markdown Cancellations

1.

Classification	Dollar Markdowns	Markdown Cancellations
	36	6
	29	6
	26	3

2.

Classification	Dollar Markdowns	Markdown Cancellations
	99.99	14.85
	63.00	41.16
	59.00	15.34

3.

Classification	Dollar Markdowns	Markdown Cancellations

4.

Classification	Dollar Markdowns	Markdown Cancellations

Chapter 6

Maintained Markup

MERCHANDISING CONCEPT 6–1: CALCULATE MAINTAINED MARKUP

The markup that is actually realized after the merchandise is sold is the *maintained markup*. Initial markup is related to the markup placed on merchandise when it first enters the store; maintained markup is concerned with the markup the store actually makes when the merchandise is sold. Because maintained markup is a measure of the actual amount of money obtained after the merchandise has been sold, it is a truer barometer of a department or store's profitability. Initial markup is only what the buyer "hoped" to obtain when the merchandise was placed on the sales floor.

The selling season must be over before maintained markup can be calculated and buyers determine the results of their planning. Retailers want to maximize profits; therefore, buyers attempt to achieve as high a markup as possible. Stores, however, must keep their markups within limits to ensure competitive pricing.

Normally, maintained markup is expressed as a percentage, not in dollars. To calculate the maintained markup percentage, buyers subtract *the cost of reductions percentage* from the initial markup percentage. In other words, the initial markup is being reduced by only the *cost* of any reductions made during that selling season as shown in Figure 6.1.

FIGURE 6.1

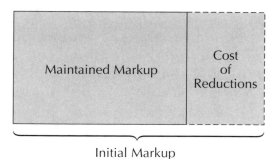

Initial Markup

First, the cost of reductions can be calculated using the following formula:

Cost of Reductions % = Reductions % × (100% − Initial Markup %)

Then, the maintained markup percentage can be calculated by using the following formula:

Maintained Markup % = Initial Markup % − Cost of Reductions %

Or, all these calculations can be placed into one formula as follows:

Maintained Markup % = Initial Markup % − [Reductions % × (100% − Initial Markup %)]

SAMPLE PROBLEM

At the end of a selling season the buyer for the toy department calculated that the following reductions (expressed as percentages) had occurred:

Markdowns	9%
Shortages	2%
Employee Discounts	3%

If the initial markup percentage had been 50 percent, what is the maintained markup percentage?

Sample Solution

Maintained Markup % = Initial Markup % −
[Reductions % − (100% − Initial Markup %)]
Maintained Markup % = .50 − ((.09 + .02 + .03) × (1.00 − .50))
Maintained Markup % = .50 − (.14 × .50)
Maintained Markup % = .50 − .07
Maintained Markup % = .43
Maintained Markup % = 43%

Using Computerized Spreadsheets

1. Using your *Merchandising CD*, follow instructions you have previously used to open file **CH06-1-1**.
2. Enter the data used in the sample problem to solve that problem.
3. Use the spreadsheet to calculate the maintained markup percentage for the problems that follow. Record all your answers on the forms for **ASSIGNMENT 6.1.1**.
4. When you have completed the lesson, **Save** the file under the file name **CH06-1-1A**, and then **Close** the file.
5. **Quit** the spreadsheet, unless you will be completing the next assignment immediately.

Assignment Problems

1. A buyer plans an initial markup of 46 percent. Reductions are expected to be 8 percent. What maintained markup can be expected?
2. A store has an initial markup of 46.9 percent. Reductions are planned at 8.1 percent. What maintained markup can be expected?
3. What is a store's maintained markup percentage if it has an initial markup of 45 percent and 11 percent reductions?
4. A shoe store with an initial markup of 49.3 percent had total reductions of 12 percent. What maintained markup was achieved?
5. A men's clothing store with an initial markup of 51.4 percent had reductions of 16 percent. What was the maintained markup percentage?

ASSIGNMENT 6.1.1

Calculating Maintained Markup

1.

Initial Markup %	
Reductions %	
Maintained Markup %	

2.

Initial Markup %	
Reductions %	
Maintained Markup %	

3.

Initial Markup %	
Reductions %	
Maintained Markup %	

4.

Initial Markup %	
Reductions %	
Maintained Markup %	

5.

Initial Markup %	
Reductions %	
Maintained Markup %	

Creating and Using Your Own Spreadsheet

1. Using your *Merchandising CD*, follow instructions you have previously used to open file **CH06-1-2**.
2. Create a spreadsheet that will allow you to enter the percentage of each reduction (markdowns, employee discounts, and shortages) separately as well as to calculate the maintained markup percentage. Your spreadsheet layout should resemble the one shown in Figure 6.2.
3. Calculate the maintained markup percentage for each of the problems that follow. Record your answers on the forms for **ASSIGNMENT 6.1.2**.
4. When you have completed the lesson, **Save** the file under the file name **CH06-1-2A**, and then **Close** the file.

FIGURE 6.2

Maintained Markup %	
Initial Markup	
Markdown	
Shortages	
Employee Discounts	
Maintained Markup %	

5. **Quit** the spreadsheet, unless you will be completing the next assignment immediately.

Assignment Problems

1. Calculate the maintained markup percentage for the following situation:

Markdowns	7.3%
Shortages	2.1%
Employee Discounts	3.6%
Initial Markup %	49.5%

2. Calculate the maintained markup percentage for the following situation:

Markdowns	5%
Shortages	1.1%
Employee Discounts	1%
Initial Markup %	44%

3. Calculate the maintained markup percentage for the following situation:

Markdowns	8%
Shortages	2.1%
Employee Discounts	2%
Initial Markup %	52%

4. A toy department had the following figures for spring: markdowns–9 percent; employee discounts–2 percent; and shortages–2 percent. If the initial markup for the department was 47.4 percent, what was the maintained markup percentage?

5. In a sporting goods department, the initial markup was 49.1 percent. Markdowns were 10 percent, and shortages were 2 percent. What was the maintained markup?

ASSIGNMENT 6.1.2
Calculating Maintained Markup

1.

Initial Markup %	
Markdown %	
Employee Discount %	
Shortages %	
Maintained Markup %	

2.

Initial Markup %	
Markdown %	
Employee Discount %	
Shortages %	
Maintained Markup %	

3.

Initial Markup %	
Markdown %	
Employee Discount %	
Shortages %	
Maintained Markup %	

4.

Initial Markup %	
Markdown %	
Employee Discount %	
Shortages %	
Maintained Markup %	

5.

Initial Markup %	
Markdown %	
Employee Discount %	
Shortages %	
Maintained Markup %	

Chapter 7

Stock Planning

MERCHANDISING CONCEPT 7–1: CALCULATE STOCK TURNOVER RATE

One of the primary goals of every retailer is to keep stock moving. Faster sales mean that new merchandise can be purchased and merchandise in stock is being sold with fewer markdowns. Decisions buyers make in relation to stock planning must yield a profit for their stores. One measure of how accurately they balance sales to inventory levels is the *stock turnover rate*. How fast merchandise is sold, replenished, and sold again determines the stock turnover for a store or department.

The stock turnover rate is defined as the number of times the average stock is sold during a period of time and is calculated using the following formula:

$$\text{Stock Turnover Rate} = \text{Sales/Average Stock}$$

Stock turnover may be determined for any period of time (for a week, a month, or an entire selling season); however, turnover usually is calculated for a one-year period.

Buyers and managers can determine a great deal about how well a store, department, or product classification is doing by knowing stock turnover rates. Like other performance measurements—such as sales, profits, and maintained markups—turnover rates of comparable retailers can be determined from trade journals or other industry publica-

FIGURE 7.1
Average Stock Turnover Rates by Departments
for Department Stores

Department	
Female Apparel	2.6
Adult Female Accessories	1.8
Men's and Boy's Apparel and Accessories	2.3
Infant's and Children's Clothing	2.7
Footwear	2.0

tions. Sample stock turnover rates for selected departments in a department store can be found in Figure 7.1.

The type of merchandise carried and store policies have an impact on stock turnover; however, almost every decision a retailer makes affects turnover. Less frequently purchased items, such as furniture and jewelry, have much lower turnover rates than do items found in grocery stores. Some store policies in regard to carrying wide assortments of merchandise in many sizes and colors will tend to cause low turnovers because some colors and sizes may not sell as well as others. For that reason, some stores carry only fast-selling colors and sizes in order to generate higher turnover rates.

Higher stock turnover rates are usually an advantage to the store or department because rapid turnover of stock reduces the number and amount of markdowns required to move dated merchandise. Merchandise that is being replaced frequently always looks fresh and has much greater appeal to the customer. However, when attempting to increase turnover, buyers must also be concerned with increased expenses, such as advertising or more salaries for additional salespeople. Both might be required to generate more sales. In these situations, increased turnover may not result in increased profits.

SAMPLE PROBLEMS

Sample Problem 1
Calculate stock turnover given the following information:

Total Sales = $60,000
Average Stock = $13,846

Sample Solution

> Stock Turnover Rate = Sales/Average Stock
> Stock Turnover Rate = $60,000/$13,846
> Stock Turnover Rate = 4.3

This means that the average stock for this department is sold and re-plenished 4.3 times during the year. The formula for stock turnover can also be rearranged algebraically to plan either sales or average stock. Many times, management may establish a stock turnover goal for buyers or department heads. If they can determine their average stock levels from past sales records, the amount of sales needed to reach the turnover goal can be calculated. First, the stock turnover formula would need to be rearranged as follows:

$$Sales = Stock\ Turnover\ Rate \times Average\ Stock$$

Now, examine the sample problem below based on this concept.

Sample Problem 2

Management has set a goal for your department to reach a stock turnover rate of 6.0. If the average stock to be carried has a value of $54,000, what will net sales need to be to reach this goal?

Sample Solution

> Sales = Stock Turnover Rate × Average Stock
> Sales = 6.0 × $54,000
> Sales = $324,000

This means that sales would need to be $324,000 if your department is to reach a stock turnover of 6.0 when carrying an average stock valued at $54,000. Examination of past sales records would help you determine if this sales amount is attainable.

Sometimes, buyers may want to determine the amount of average stock that would be required to reach a predetermined stock turnover rate. In such a situation, they must be able to estimate sales based on past store records. First, the stock turnover formula would need to be rearranged as follows:

$$Average\ Stock = Sales/Stock\ Turnover\ Rate$$

Examine the sample problem below based on this concept.

Sample Problem 3

A department plans sales of $100,000 with an estimated stock turnover rate of 3. Based on these estimates, what will average stock need to be?

Sample Solution

> Average Stock = Sales/Stock Turnover Rate
> Average Stock = $100,000/3
> Average Stock = $33,333

This calculation indicates to the buyer that average stock must be valued at $33,333 if both the sales and stock turnover goals are to be reached.

Using Computerized Spreadsheets

Buyers can use the stock turnover formula to make any of the calculations previously described. Using a spreadsheet would allow them to ask "what if" for many different situations and still be able to perform the calculations quickly.

1. Using your *Merchandising CD*, follow instructions you have previously used to open file **CH07-1-1**. All three calculations that you have reviewed have already been set up as shown in Figure 7.2.

FIGURE 7.2

Calculate Stock Turnover	Total Sales	$60,000.00
	Average Stock	$13,846.00
	Stock Turnover Rate	4.3
Calculate Sales	Stock Turnover Rate	6.0
	Average Stock	$54,000.00
	Sales	$324,000.00
Calculate Average Stock	Sales	$100,000.00
	Stock Turnover Rate	3.0
	Average Stock	$33,333.33

2. Use the spreadsheet to complete the problems that follow. Record all your answers on the form for **ASSIGNMENT 7.1.1**.

3. When you have completed the lesson, **Save** the file under the file name **CH07-1-1A**, and then **Close** the file.

4. **Quit** the spreadsheet, unless you will be completing the next assignment immediately.

Assignment Problems

1. A department had annual sales of $224,000. The average stock carried a retail value of $86,154. What was the stock turnover rate?

2. This year, the department head feels sales will increase to $230,000. Management has established a stock turnover goal of 2.8 for the department. What will average stock need to be to reach this goal?

3. The department head feels that sales will remain stable at $224,000 during the coming year. Several slow-selling lines will be eliminated from inventory, causing the value of average stock to be reduced to $81,999. Based on this information, calculate the stock turnover rate.

4. If sales for the department remain at $224,000 and management wants an increase in the stock turnover rate to 2.9, what average stock is required?

5. From industry sources, a buyer for women's apparel has determined that the average stock turnover rate is 3.8. If annual sales of $750,000 are planned, what average stock is required?

6. For the information presented in problem 5, calculate average stock if sales were planned at $800,000.

7. After examining local conditions, the buyer believes that a stock turnover rate of 3.8 is not attainable this year. If the buyer lowers that goal to 3.5 and continues to plan sales at $750,000, what average stock is required?

8. A stationery store plans a stock turnover rate of 3.5. If the average stock is planned at $54,320, what sales will be required to achieve this goal?

9. The buyer for the infant's department has a stock turnover goal of 2.9. With an average stock of $26,987, what sales would be required to achieve this goal?

10. If the stock turnover goal remains 2.9 and average stock is increased to $28,900, what sales would then be required?

ASSIGNMENT 7.1.1
Calculating Stock Turnover Rate

Problem	Sales	Average Stock	Stock Turnover Rate
1.			
2.			
3.			
4.			
5.			
6.			
7.			
8.			
9.			
10.			

Creating and Using Your Own Spreadsheet

The key to accurately calculating the stock turnover rate is having a reliable average stock figure. To obtain an accurate picture of stock conditions for the entire year, most retailers use beginning-of-the-month (BOM) inventory figures as well as the end-of-the-month (EOM) inventory for the last month of the year. Using this calculation thus requires 13 stock figures. In the problems that you just completed, both average stock and annual sales were given in the problem; however, each one can easily be calculated if monthly inventory and sales figures are available.

1. Using your *Merchandising CD*, follow instructions you have previously used to open file **CH07-1-2.**
2. Construct a spreadsheet that would allow you to input 12 monthly inventory and sales figures as well as an ending inventory figure for the year. Then, design a formula that will allow you to calculate the stock turnover rate.
3. First, type all your titles. Three that you probably should have would be "Month," "Retail Stock," and "Sales." Under the "Month" column, type the numbers **1** through **13**. Numbers 1 to 12 will be beginning monthly inventories and number 13 would be the ending inventory for December. In the 14th row below the heading "Month," type the word **Totals.** You will also need to label a cell "Stock Turnover Rate." You will need formulas to calculate each of the following:

FIGURE 7.3

Calculate Stock Turnover		
Month	Retail Stock	Sales
1		
2		
3		
4		
5		
6		
7		
8		
9		
10		
11		
12		
EOM Inventory		
TOTALS		
Stock Turnover Rate		

- Total average inventory that can be calculated by adding inventory figures and dividing by 13.
- Total annual sales that can be calculated by adding the monthly sales.
- Annual stock turnover that can be calculated by dividing the annual sales figure by the average stock figure.

4. Your spreadsheet layout should resemble the one shown in Figure 7.3. Use the spreadsheet to complete the problems that follow. Record all your answers on the forms for **ASSIGNMENT 7.1.2.**

5. When you have completed the lesson, **Save** the file under the file name **CH07-1-2A**, and then **Close** the file.

6. **Quit** the spreadsheet, unless you will be completing the next assignment immediately.

Assignment Problems

1. Calculate the stock turnover rate based on the following monthly sales and inventory figures:

Month	Sales	Retail Stock
1	$10,000	$28,000
2	$11,000	$32,000
3	$13,000	$34,000
4	$16,000	$37,000
5	$19,000	$34,000
6	$9,000	$19,000
7	$11,000	$32,000
8	$13,000	$34,000
9	$16,000	$37,000
10	$19,000	$34,000
11	$21,000	$29,000
12	$25,000	$34,000
EOM		$21,000

2. Calculate the stock turnover rate based on the following monthly sales and inventory figures:

Month	Sales	Retail Stock
1	$11,686	$18,979
2	$12,535	$18,755
3	$14,889	$22,678
4	$15,756	$22,545
5	$14,342	$20,698
6	$13,676	$17,834
7	$15,889	$23,678
8	$16,756	$23,545
9	$15,342	$21,698
10	$14,676	$18,834
11	$16,889	$24,678
12	$17,756	$24,545
EOM		$21,657

ASSIGNMENT 7.1.2

Calculating Stock Turnover Rate

1.

Total Sales	
Total Retail Stock	
Stock Turnover Rate	

2.

Total Sales	
Total Retail Stock	
Stock Turnover Rate	

MERCHANDISING CONCEPT 7–2: CALCULATE STOCK-TO-SALES RATIO AND PLANNED SALES

Merchandise in stock must be sufficient to meet sales expectations while allowing for unanticipated demand. A buyer's goal will be to maintain an inventory assortment that will be sufficient to meet customer demand, yet be small enough to ensure a reasonable return on the store's investment in inventory. One of the most often used methods of inventory planning is using the *stock-to-sales ratio method*, which involves maintaining inventory in a specific ratio to sales for a stated period of time—usually on a monthly basis. Stock-to-sales ratios are calculated by dividing the dollar value of stock by actual sales in dollars.

The stock-to-sales ratio indicates the relationship between planned sales and the amount of stock required to produce those sales. Industry-wide stock-to-sales ratios, like the ones shown in Figure 7.4, are

FIGURE 7.4
Average Monthly Stock-to-Sales Ratios for Department Stores

Month	Stock-to-Sales Ratio
January	6.10
February	5.41
March	4.99
April	5.03
May	5.07
June	4.92
July	5.41
August	4.81
September	4.63
October	5.33
November	4.44
December	2.78

available from sources such as the National Retail Federation and Dun & Bradstreet. Buyers can also calculate stock-to-sales ratios for their store or department based on previous stock levels and sales figures.

SAMPLE PROBLEM

If a department had merchandise valued at $40,000 to begin the month of April and sales were $20,000, what would be the stock-to-sales ratio?

Sample Solution:

Stock-to-Sales Ratio = Value of Stock/Actual Sales
Stock-to-Sales Ratio = $40,000/$20,000
Stock-to-Sales Ratio = 2

This calculation indicates that for every item sold there must be two in stock. In other words, there must be two dollars invested in inventory for every dollar in sales.

Using Computerized Spreadsheets

1. Using your *Merchandising CD*, follow instructions you have previously used to open file **CH07-2-1**. The spreadsheet has already been designed for you.
2. Use the spreadsheet to complete the problems that follow. Record all your answers on the forms for **ASSIGNMENT 7.2.1.**
3. When you have completed the lesson, **Save** the file under the file name **CH07-2-1A**, and then **Close** the file.
4. **Quit** the spreadsheet, unless you will be completing the next assignment immediately.

Assignment Problems

1. Use the spreadsheet to calculate the stock-to-sales ratio for each of the months that follow:

Month	Month Sales	Retail Stock
1	$11,686	$18,979
2	$12,535	$18,755
3	$14,889	$22,678

4	$15,756	$22,545
5	$14,342	$20,698
6	$13,676	$17,834
7	$15,889	$23,678
8	$16,756	$23,545
9	$15,342	$21,698
10	$14,676	$18,834
11	$16,889	$24,678
12	$17,756	$24,545

2. A department manager had sales of $25,000 and a beginning inventory of $80,000 for the month of June. Calculate the stock-to-sales ratio.
3. Beginning inventory was $115,000, and sales for the period were $51,600. What was the stock-to-sales ratio?
4. Beginning inventory for the month was $36,900, and sales were $25,000. Calculate the stock-to-sales ratio.

ASSIGNMENT 7.2.1

Calculating Stock-to-Sales Ratio

1.

Month	BOM Stock	Sales	Stock-to-Sales Ratio
1			
2			
3			
4			
5			
6			
7			
8			
9			
10			
11			
12			

Problem	BOM Stock	Sales	Stock-to-Sales Ratio
2			
3			
4			

Creating and Using Your Own Spreadsheet

The formula for calculating the stock-to-sales ratio can also be used to plan beginning inventory. Many times, buyers will know what the stock-to-sales ratio should be for a department if they have tracked the ratio for their department or product category over a period of years. By multiplying planned sales by the stock-to-sales ratio, buyers can calculate what their beginning inventory should be. The following formula is used:

BOM Stock = Stock-to-Sales Ratio × Planned Sales

For example, in September the stock-to-sales ratio for a department is planned at 2.8. If the buyer plans sales of $50,000, beginning stock levels can be calculated. Multiplying 2.8 times $50,000 indicates to the buyer that $140,000 worth of merchandise needs to be on hand at the beginning of the month.

1. Using your *Merchandising CD*, follow instructions you have previously used to open file **CH07-2-2**.
2. Construct a spreadsheet that would allow you to input a stock-to-sales ratio and a planned sales figure. Then, design a formula that will allow you to calculate BOM stock based on these two figures.
3. First, type all your titles before you enter your formula.
4. Use the spreadsheet to answer the problems that follow. Record all your answers on the forms for **ASSIGNMENT 7.2.2.**
5. When you have completed the lesson, **Save** the file under the file name **CH07-2-2A**, and then **Close** the file.
6. **Quit** the spreadsheet, unless you will be completing the next assignment immediately.

Assignment Problems

A buyer has planned sales for each of the next six months. Stock-to-sales ratios have been calculated based on past store records. Using this information, calculate planned BOM stock for each month.

Planned Sales	Stock-to-Sales Ratio
1. $16,000	2.4
2. $19,000	2.1
3. $ 9,000	2.1
4. $45,000	2.0
5. $49,500	2.0

ASSIGNMENT 7.2.2

Calculating BOM Stock Using Stock-to-Sales Ratio

1.

Planned Sales	
Stock-to-Sales Ratio	
BOM Stock	

2.

Planned Sales	
Stock-to-Sales Ratio	
BOM Stock	

3.

Planned Sales	
Stock-to-Sales Ratio	
BOM Stock	

4.

Planned Sales	
Stock-to-Sales Ratio	
BOM Stock	

5.

Planned Sales	
Stock-to-Sales Ratio	
BOM Stock	

Chapter 8

Planning Sales and Purchases

MERCHANDISING CONCEPT 8–1:
CALCULATE PLANNED SALES

Most retailers will use a six-month plan to represent their planning ef-
forts. Key components of every plan include sales forecasts and stock
planning. The *six-month merchandise plan* is the tool that translates
profit objectives into a framework for merchandising planning and control. A sample six-month merchandise plan is shown in Figure 8.1.

The first and most important part of the six-month merchandise plan
is forecasting sales. All other merchandising decisions are planned in
relation to sales or stated as a percentage of sales. Therefore, if the sales
forecast is inaccurate, all the other parts of the plan will be in error,
possibly causing disastrous results for the retailer. Last year's sales usually provide the basis for determining planned sales for the current year;
however, buyers should also examine previous years' sales figures. Usually buyers are able to detect an upward or downward trend in sales,
but what happens this year will depend on whether or not conditions
are similar to past conditions.

Once total sales are planned for a six-month period, this sales figure
must be distributed over the six-month period. In other words, buyers
must estimate what percentage of total sales will occur during each
month of the period. Usually these distribution percentages remain relatively stable over time; however, both internal and external conditions
can cause changes to occur. For example, the Easter holiday occurs in

FIGURE 8.1

		PLAN (This Year)	ACTUAL (Last Year)
	Dept Name _____ Dept No. _____		

<table>
<tr><td rowspan="8">SIX-MONTH MERCHANDISING PLAN</td><td></td><td>PLAN
(This Year)</td><td>ACTUAL
(Last Year)</td></tr>
<tr><td>Workroom cost</td><td></td><td></td></tr>
<tr><td>Cash discount %</td><td></td><td></td></tr>
<tr><td>Season stock turnover</td><td></td><td></td></tr>
<tr><td>Shortage %</td><td></td><td></td></tr>
<tr><td>Average Stock</td><td></td><td></td></tr>
<tr><td>Markdown %</td><td></td><td></td></tr>
</table>

SPRING 20 ____		FEB	MAR	APR	MAY	JUNE	JULY	SEASON TOTAL
FALL 20 ____		AUG	SEP	OCT	NOV	DEC	JAN	
SALES $	Last Year							
	Plan							
	% of Increase							
	Revised							
	Actual							
RETAIL STOCK (BOM)	Last Year							
	Plan							
	Revised							
	Actual							
RETAIL STOCK (EOM)	Last Year							
	Plan							
	Revised							
	Actual							
REDUCTIONS $	Last Year							
	Plan							
	Revised							
	Actual							
PURCHASES AT RETAIL	Last Year							
	Plan							
	Revised							
	Actual							
PURCHASES AT COST	Last Year							
	Plan							
	Revised							
	Actual							

Comments _____

Merchandise Manager _____ Buyer _____
Controller _____

either April or March, or their store may be planning on changes in marketing strategies during a specific month that did not occur in the past. If buyers determine that such factors will have an impact on the percentage of sales occurring each month, they must adjust the planned sales percentage for each month.

SAMPLE PROBLEM

For planning purposes, you have assumed that the percentage of total sales for the period occurring each month will remain the same as last year. Those figures are listed below:

February	12%
March	14%
April	26%
May	21%
June	14%
July	13%

After carefully analyzing past sales records and current market conditions, you have estimated that a 10 percent increase in sales will occur this season. Last year's sales for the same six-month period were $87,000. Based on this information, plan sales for each month listed above.

Sample Solution

First, you need to calculate total planned sales for the six-month period. Multiply the planned sales increase by the total sales for last year (.10 × $87,000 = $8,700). Then, add the planned increase in sales to last year's sales ($87,000 + $8,700 = $95,700). This year's total planned sales for the period are $95,700. (*Note*: Planned sales could also have been calculated in one step by multiplying by 1.10).

Next, using the planned percentage of total sales for each month and the planned total sales figure, you would make the following calculations:

Month	Monthly % of Total Sales		Planned Sales		Monthly Sales
February	12%	×	$95,700	=	$11,484
March	14%	×	$95,700	=	$13,398
April	26%	×	$95,700	=	$24,882
May	21%	×	$95,700	=	$20,097
June	14%	×	$95,700	=	$13,398
July	13%	×	$95,700	=	$12,441

Using Computerized Spreadsheets

1. Using your *Merchandising CD*, follow instructions you have previously used to open file **CH08-1-1**.

2. Use the spreadsheet that has already been prepared to complete the problems that follow. Record all your answers on the forms for **ASSIGNMENT 8.1.1**.

3. When you have completed the lesson, **Save** the file under the file name **CH08-1-1A**, and then **Close** the file.

4. **Quit** the spreadsheet, unless you will be completing the next assignment immediately.

Assignment Problems

1. Sales last year for your store were $168,421. What will be planned sales for this year, if you anticipated a 6 percent increase in sales?

2. After making the calculation for problem 1, you read in the newspaper that the largest factory in town was laying off half its workforce. You have decided to adjust your planned sales increase to only 2 percent. Now, what will be your planned sales?

3. What if you had read that a major competitor had decided to leave your market area? You probably would adjust your planned sales increase upward. What will be your planned sales if a 15 percent increase is anticipated?

4. Sales last year were $268,720. What will be planned sales for this year, if you anticipated a 4.5 percent increase in sales?

5. If last year's sales were $234,790, what will be planned sales for this year with an increase in sales anticipated at 3.9 percent?

ASSIGNMENT 8.1.1
Calculating Planned Sales

1.

Sales (LY)	
% Change	
Planned Sales	

2.

Sales (LY)	
% Change	
Planned Sales	

3.

Sales (LY)	
% Change	
Planned Sales	

4.

Sales (LY)	
% Change	
Planned Sales	

5.

Sales (LY)	
% Change	
Planned Sales	

Creating and Using Your Own Spreadsheet

1. Using your *Merchandising CD*, follow instructions you have previously used to open file **CH08-1-2**. Your goal is to design a spreadsheet that will allocate total planned sales by month for a six-month period. Here are a few hints on getting started:
   - In column 1, type the title **Month**. Below this heading, type the names of the six months beginning with February and ending with July.
   - In column 2, type the title **% of Sales.**
   - In column 3, type the title **Monthly Sales.** Under column 3, establish a formula for each of the six months that will calculate monthly sales based on a percentage of total planned sales.
2. Your completed spreadsheet layout should resemble the one shown in Figure 8.2. Use the spreadsheet you have designed to calculate planned

FIGURE 8.2

PLANNED SALES		
Sales Last Year		
Anticipated Increase		
Planned Sales		$0.00
Month	% of Sales	Monthly Sales
February		
March		
April		
May		
June		
July		

monthly sales for the problems that follow. Record all your answers on the forms for **ASSIGNMENT 8.1.2**.

3. When you have completed the lesson, **Save** the file under the file name **CH08-1-2A**, and then **Close** the file.

4. **Quit** the spreadsheet, unless you will be completing the next assignment immediately.

Assignment Problems

1. Sales last year for your store were $168,421. This year you anticipate a 6 percent increase in sales. Calculate monthly planned sales if planned sales distribution for each month is as follows:

February	10%
March	20%
April	30%
May	20%
June	10%
July	10%

2. After examining your planned monthly sales figures, your merchandise manager sent back the following monthly revisions based on new planned in-store promotions:

February	12%
March	18%
April	35%
May	15%
June	10%
July	10%

Calculate planned monthly sales based on these new estimates.

3. You just realized that Easter will occur in March this year, rather than in April, as it did last year. You once again adjust your monthly sales estimates as follows:

February	12%
March	30%
April	18%
May	20%
June	10%
July	10%

Calculate planned monthly sales based on these changes.

4. Sales last year were $268,720. A 4.5 percent sales increase is anticipated this year. Calculate monthly planned sales if planned sales distribution for each month is as follows:

February	10%
March	20%
April	30%
May	20%
June	10%
July	10%

5. Last year's sales were $234,790, and a 3.9 percent sales increase is anticipated this year. Calculate monthly planned sales if planned sales distribution for each month is as follows:

February	10%
March	20%
April	30%
May	20%
June	10%
July	10%

ASSIGNMENT 8.1.2

Calculating Planned Sales

1.

Month	Planned Monthly Sales
February	
March	
April	
May	
June	
July	

2.

Month	Planned Monthly Sales
February	
March	
April	
May	
June	
July	

3.

Month	Planned Monthly Sales
February	
March	
April	
May	
June	
July	

4.

Month	Planned Monthly Sales
February	
March	
April	
May	
June	
July	

5.

Month	Planned Monthly Sales
February	
March	
April	
May	
June	
July	

MERCHANDISING CONCEPT 8–2:
CALCULATE PLANNED PURCHASES

Whether buyers are purchasing fashion or basic merchandise, they must plan and control merchandise purchases. Planning is essential to provide direction and serve as a basis of control for any store or department. Integrally related to planning is the necessity of controlling merchandising decisions. Buyers must check their plans periodically to ensure they are being followed and achieving the desired results. Most retailers develop merchandise plans for the entire store as well as specific departments and product classifications. These merchandise plans provide for an effective control over purchases and tend to prevent the department or store from becoming overstocked or understocked.

Planned purchases can be calculated for any period of time, but many retailers plan purchases for a six-month period.

Enough merchandise must be purchased to cover (1) sales for the period, (2) desired ending stock for the period, and (3) all reductions (markdowns, employee/customer discounts, and shortages). However, the amount of merchandise already on hand must be subtracted from these inventory needs.

Planned purchases represent the merchandise that is to be purchased during any given period. Planned purchases are calculated by using the following formula:

Planned Purchases = Planned Sales + Planned Reductions + Planned Ending Inventory (EOM)
− Planned Beginning Inventory (BOM)

SAMPLE PROBLEM

The buyer for Department A wants to plan purchases for the coming month. Based on past sales records and an analysis of market conditions, sales are estimated to be $22,000. Reductions planned for the month total $2,000. An ending inventory valued at $35,000 is planned. If beginning inventory had a value of $33,000, what are planned purchases for the month?

Sample Solution

Planned Purchases = Planned Sales + Planned Reductions + Planned
Ending Inventory (EOM) − Planned Beginning Inventory (BOM)
Planned Purchases = $22,000 + $2,000 + $35,000 − $33,000
Planned Purchases = $26,000

This calculation indicates that the buyer will have to spend $26,000 (at retail) on merchandise during the month in order to reach the beginning inventory level for the following month.

Using Computerized Spreadsheets

1. Using your *Merchandising CD*, follow instructions you have previously used to open file **CH08-2-1**.
2. Use the spreadsheet that has already been established to calculate planned purchases for each of the problems that follow. Record all your answers on the form for **ASSIGNMENT 8.2.1**.

3. When you have completed the lesson, **Save** the file under the file name **CH08-2-1A**, and then **Close** the file.
4. **Quit** the spreadsheet, unless you will be completing the next assignment immediately.

Assignment Problems

1. For the month of October, the shoe department planned sales of $20,000. The beginning inventory was $51,200. Planned ending inventory is $41,500. What would planned purchases be if reductions are planned at:
   a. $1,000
   b. $1,500
   c. $500
2. Planned sales are $42,000 with a planned ending inventory of $81,000. Reductions are estimated at $3,000. What would planned purchases be:
   a. If beginning inventory was $78,235.
   b. If sales increase to $48,500.
   c. If sales are planned at $38,000.
3. For the month of April, planned sales were $41,500 and estimated markdowns were $3,800. Beginning inventory is $82,598. What would planned purchases be if ending inventory is:
   a. $86,500
   b. $90.000
   c. $84,000
4. To begin the month, a buyer has a beginning inventory of $25,752. For the month, sales of $13,500 are planned with an ending inventory of $28,700. Calculate planned purchases for the month.

For all the problems that you just completed, planned purchases were calculated at retail. Usually, buyers will also want to calculate planned purchases at cost. Planned purchases at cost represent the amount of money that the buyer expects to spend on merchandise purchases during a given period of time. Planned purchases at cost are calculated using the following formula:

Planned Purchases at Cost = Planned Purchases at Retail × (100% − Initial Markup %)

ASSIGNMENT 8.2.1
Calculating Planned Purchases

Problem	Sales	Reductions	EOM	BOM	Planned Purchases
1-a.					
1-b.					
1-c.					
2-a.					
2-b.					
2-c.					
3-a.					
3-b.					
3-c.					
4.					

Creating and Using Your Own Spreadsheet

1. Using your *Merchandising CD*, follow instructions you have previously used to open file **CH08-2-2**. Set up a formula that will allow you to calculate planned purchases at cost by using the "Planned Purchase at Retail" figure you are already calculating.

2. Type the titles **Markup %** and **Purchases at Cost.** In the cell to the right of the title "Purchases at Cost," construct a formula that will allow you to calculate planned purchases at cost based on previous entries and calculations on the spreadsheet.

3. Your completed spreadsheet layout should resemble the one shown in Figure 8.3. Use the spreadsheet to calculate planned purchases at cost for the problems that follow. Record all your answers on the form for **ASSIGNMENT 8.2.2**.

4. When you have completed the lesson, **Save** the file under the file name **CH08-2-2A**, and then **Close** the file.

5. **Quit** the spreadsheet, unless you will be completing the next assignment immediately.

Assignment Problems

1. For the month of October, sales in the shoe department are planned at $20,000. The beginning inventory is $51,200. Reductions are planned

FIGURE 8.3

PLANNED PURCHASES	
Sales	
Reductions	
EOM	
BOM	
Planned Purchases	$0.00
Markup %	
Purchases at Cost	

at $1,000, and planned ending inventory is $41,500. What would planned purchases at cost be if the initial markup percentage is:

a. 47.3%

b. 49.1%

c. 46.6%

2. An ending inventory of $81,000 is planned for a department. Reductions are estimated at $3,000. Beginning inventory is $78,235. If a 42.9 percent initial markup is used, what are planned purchases at cost if planned sales are:

a. $41,500

b. $48,000

c. $38,000

3. For the month of April, planned sales were $41,500, and estimated markdowns were $3,800. Ending inventory is planned at $86,500. Beginning inventory is $82,598. What are planned purchases at cost for the initial markup percentages that follow?

a. 46.9%

b. 45%

c. 49.9%

4. To begin the month, a buyer has a beginning inventory of $25,752. For the month, sales of $13,500 are planned, with an ending inventory of $28,700. Calculate planned purchases at cost if a 42.1 percent initial markup is used.

| ASSIGNMENT 8.2.2 | | | | |

Calculating Planned Purchases

Problem	Sales	Reductions	EOM	BOM	Planned Purchases at Cost
1-a.					
1-b.					
1-c.					
2-a.					
2-b.					
2-c.					
3-a.					
3-b.					
3-c.					
4.					

MERCHANDISING CONCEPT 8–3: DEVELOP A SIX-MONTH MERCHANDISE BUYING PLAN

A six-month merchandise plan translates profit objectives into a framework for merchandise planning and control. Most retailers have different forms for developing the six-month merchandise buying plan, but generally they contain the following elements:

- **Initial Markup**. Goals will be indicated as to the desired markup that should be placed on merchandise when it enters the store.
- **Planned Net Sales**. Planned net sales represent gross sales minus customer returns and allowances. Last year's sales usually provide the basis for determining planned sales for the current year; however, buyers must determine the percentage by which they estimate past sales will either increase or decline. All changes affecting the store, both internally and externally, must be examined carefully before this decision can be made.
- **Planned Beginning-of-the-Month (BOM) Inventory**. There must be adequate stock to achieve the planned sales. The relationship between the amount of stock in the store and planned sales is most frequently calculated using the stock-to-sales ratio method of stock planning.
- **Planned End-of-the-Month (EOM) Inventory**. Planned EOM inventory represents the retail value of the ending inventory for each period. On a merchandising plan form, the beginning inventory for a period (BOM) must be the value of the ending inventory (EOM) for the preceding period.

- **Planned Reductions**. The total of planned markdowns, shortages, and employee/customer discounts must also be entered into the merchandise plan. Dollar amounts for these items can be calculated using planned percentage-of-sales figures.
- **Planned Purchases at Retail**. Planned purchases at retail represent the retail value of merchandise that is to be purchased during a given period. Planned purchases at retail are calculated using the first formula described in Merchandising Concept 8–2.
- **Planned Purchases at Cost**. Planned purchases at cost represent the amount of money that the buyer expects to spend on merchandise purchases during a given period. Planned purchases at cost are calculated by using the second formula described in Merchandising Concept 8–2.

The six-month merchandise plan is one of the buyer's most important planning and control tools. Because it shows buyers the amount they should spend on new stock purchases to achieve planned sales, the merchandise plan keeps them from overspending or not achieving planned goals for the store or department.

SAMPLE PROBLEM

A buyer is in the process of developing a six-month merchandise buying plan for Department B. Last year, sales were $100,000 for the same six-month period. This year the buyer is estimating that sales will increase by 6 percent. Over the season, sales are anticipated in the following percentages:

February	12%
March	14%
April	26%
May	21%
June	14%
July	13%

A 2:1 stock-to-sales ratio is estimated for each month and will be used for inventory planning purposes. The buyer desires the ending inventory for the six-month period to be $25,000. Reductions for the season are planned at 8 percent of sales. Forty percent of the reductions are planned for June, and 60 percent are planned for July. Based on a 45 percent initial markup, develop a six-month merchandise buying plan. You will need to calculate the following:

- Planned sales for the entire six months.
- Planned sales for each month.
- Planned BOM stock levels.
- Planned reductions for the entire six months.
- Planned reductions for each month.
- Planned EOM stock levels.
- Planned purchases (at retail) for each month.
- Planned purchases (at cost) for each month.

Sample Solution

Step 1. Calculate planned sales for the period by adding the amount of the anticipated increase in sales to last year's sales for the same period. A $6,000 increase in sales is anticipated ($100,000 × .06 = $6,000.) This year, total planned sales for the period are $106,000 ($100,000 + $6,000 = $106,000). This calculation can be completed in one step on your calculator or computer by multiplying sales times (1 + % Sales Increase).

Step 2. Calculate sales for each month by multiplying planned sales for the period times the percentage of sales anticipated to occur during each month.

Month	% of Total Sales		Planned Sales		Monthly Sales
February	12%	×	$106,000	=	$12,720
March	14%	×	$106,000	=	$14,840
April	26%	×	$106,000	=	$27,560
May	21%	×	$106,000	=	$22,260
June	14%	×	$106,000	=	$14,840
July	13%	×	$106,000	=	$13,780

Step 3. Calculate the planned BOM for each month by multiplying planned monthly sales by the desired stock-to-sales ratio.

Month	Monthly Sales		Stock-to-Sales Ratio		Planned BOM
February	$12,720	×	2.1	=	$26,712
March	$14,840	×	2.1	=	$31,364
April	$27,560	×	2.1	=	$57,876
May	$22,260	×	2.1	=	$46,746
June	$14,840	×	2.1	=	$31,164
July	$13,780	×	2.1	=	$28,938

Step 4. Calculate total reductions planned for the six-month period. Reductions are planned at 8 percent of sales; therefore, reductions for the period will total $6,360 (.08 × $106,000).

Step 5. Calculate reductions planned for each month in the season as follows:

Month	Monthly Reductions		Total Reductions		Planned Reductions
February	.00	×	$6,360	=	$000.00
March	.00	×	$6,360	=	$000.00
April	.00	×	$6,360	=	$000.00
May	.00	×	$6,360	=	$000.00
June	.40	×	$6,360	=	$2,544.00
July	.60	×	$6,360	=	$3,816.00

Step 6. Determine planned ending inventory for each month. Planned ending inventory for the month will be the same as planned beginning-of-the-month (BOM) inventory for the following month. You have already made these calculations; they are as follows:

Month	Planned EOM
February	$31,364 (BOM for March)
March	$57,876 (BOM for April)
April	$46,746 (BOM for May)
May	$31,164 (BOM for June)
June	$28,938 (BOM for July)
July	$25,000 (planned EOM for the period)

Step 7. Calculate planned purchases at retail (for each month) by using the following formula:

Planned Purchases = Planned Sales + Planned Reductions + Planned Ending Inventory (EOM)
− Planned Beginning Inventory (BOM)

Month	Planned Sales		Planned Reductions		Planned EOM		Planned BOM		Planned Purchases
February	$12,720	+	$0	+	$31,364	−	$26,712	=	$17,372
March	$14,840	+	$0	+	$57,876	−	$31,364	=	$41,352
April	$27,560	+	$0	+	$46,746	−	$57,876	=	$16,430
May	$22,260	+	$0	+	$31,164	−	$46,746	=	$6,678
June	$14,840	+	$3,392	+	$28,938	−	$31,164	=	$16,006
July	$13,780	+	$5,088	+	$25,000	−	$28,938	=	$14,930

Step 8. Calculate planned purchases at cost.

Month	Planned Purchases at Retail		Cost Percent		Planned Purchases at Cost
February	$17,372	×	(100% − 45%)	=	$9,445
March	$41,352	×	(100% − 45%)	=	$22,744
April	$16,430	×	(100% − 45%)	=	$9,037
May	$6,678	×	(100% − 45%)	=	$3,673
June	$16,006	×	(100% − 45%)	=	$8,803
July	$14,930	×	(100% − 45%)	=	$8,212

The planned purchases at cost let buyers know how much money they will have to spend on merchandise for the season as well as individual months.

Using Computerized Spreadsheets

With calculations as complex as these, using computerized spreadsheets saves enormous amounts of time and allows buyers to make calculations for many different similar situations by asking "what if?"

1. Using your *Merchandising CD*, follow instructions you have previously used to open file **CH08-3**.
2. Use the spreadsheet already prepared to calculate (1) planned monthly sales, (2) planned monthly BOM, (3) planned monthly EOM, and (4) planned monthly reductions for the following situations. A sample screen is shown in Figure 8.4. Record all your answers on the forms for **ASSIGNMENT 8.3**.
3. When you have completed the lesson, **Save** the file under the file name **CH08-3A**, and then **Close** the file.
4. **Quit** the spreadsheet, unless you will be completing the next assignment immediately.

Assignment Problems

1. Last year's sales for the six-month period of February to July were $589,345. A 4.5 percent increase in sales is anticipated this year. Total reductions for the period are planned at 9 percent. The initial markup is planned at 53.7 percent. The buyer desires an ending inventory of

FIGURE 8.4

6-MONTH BUYING PLAN						
Sales (LY)						
% Planned Increase						
Planned Sales						
Planned EOM						
Initial Markup %						
Planned Reductions						
	FEB	MAR	APR	MAY	JUNE	JULY
Sales Distribution						
Stock-to-Sales Ratio						
Reductions Distribution						
PLANNED SALES						
PLANNED BOM						
PLANNED EOM						
PLANNED REDUCTIONS						

$190,000 for the period. Based on an analysis of past sales records and current market trends, the buyer has also made plans for the period in relation to (1) monthly distribution of sales, (2) monthly stock-to-sales ratios, and (3) monthly distribution of planned reductions. These three planning estimates for each month are presented below:

Month	Sales Distribution	Stock-to-Sales Ratio	Reductions Distribution
Feb	10%	2.4	5%
Mar	10%	2.4	5%
Apr	35%	2.1	10%
May	20%	2.0	20%
June	15%	2.0	30%
July	10%	2.0	30%

Calculate (1) planned monthly sales, (2) planned monthly BOM, (3) planned monthly EOM, and (4) planned monthly reductions.

2. For the information presented in problem 1, you have decided that changes must be made in only the sales distribution estimates. Recal-

culate your answers based on the following changes in sales distribution:

Feb	12%
Mar	13%
Apr	30%
May	22%
June	13%
July	10%

3. Using all the original estimates presented in problem 1 except the stock-to-sales ratios, make recalculations based on the following changes in planned stock-to-sales ratios:

Feb	2.3
Mar	2.3
Apr	2.0
May	2.0
June	2.0
July	2.0

4. Using all the original estimates presented in problem 1 except the planned distribution of reductions, make recalculations based on the following changes in planned distribution of reductions:

Feb	0%
Mar	0%
Apr	15%
May	25%
June	30%
July	30%

5. Using all the original estimates presented in problem 1 except the figure for total planned reductions, recalculate your planned monthly figures if total planned reductions are increased to 13 percent.

Creating and Using Your Own Spreadsheet

1. Using your *Merchandising CD*, follow instructions you have previously used to open file **CH08-3**. Add formulas to the spreadsheet that has already been prepared that will calculate (1) monthly planned purchases at retail, and (2) monthly planned purchases at cost.

2. Type titles for each of these calculations in the first column. Then, under each month you will need to design formulas that will make the desired monthly calculations for each of the six months as well as totals for the period.

3. Once you have established all the formulas that you need, use your new spreadsheet to complete the problems that follow. Record all your answers on the forms for **ASSIGNMENT 8.3**.

4. When you have completed the lesson, **Save** the file under the file name **CH08-3A**, and then **Close** the file.

5. **Quit** the spreadsheet, unless you will be completing the next assignment immediately.

Assignment Problems

6. Last year's sales for the six-month period of February to July were $356,900. A 5.5 percent increase in sales is anticipated this year. Total reductions for the period are planned at 8 percent. The buyer desires an ending inventory of $115,000 for the period. A 48 percent initial markup is planned. Based on an analysis of past sales records and current market trends, a buyer has also made plans for the period in relation to (1) monthly distribution of sales, (2) monthly stock-to-sales ratios, and (3) monthly distribution of planned reductions. Those planning estimates are presented below:

Month	Sales Distribution	Stock-to-Sales Ratio	Reductions Distribution
Feb	10%	2.4	5%
Mar	10%	2.4	5%
Apr	35%	2.1	10%
May	20%	2.0	20%
June	15%	2.0	30%
July	10%	2.0	30%

Calculate: (1) planned monthly sales, (2) planned monthly BOM, (3) planned monthly EOM, (4) planned monthly reductions, (5) planned monthly purchases at retail, and (6) planned monthly purchases at cost.

7. Based on the information presented in problem 6, make recalculations for all monthly figures based on the following changes in sales distribution:

Feb	12%
Mar	13%
Apr	30%
May	22%
June	13%
July	10%

8. Based on the information presented in problem 6, make recalculations for all monthly figures based on the following changes in planned stock-to-sales ratios:

Feb	2.3
Mar	2.3
Apr	2.0
May	2.0
June	2.0
July	2.0

9. Based on the information presented in problem 6, make recalculations for all monthly figures based on the following changes in planned distribution of reductions:

Feb	0%
Mar	0%
Apr	15%
May	25%
June	30%
July	30%

10. Recalculate your planned monthly figures for the information presented in problem 6 if the initial markup is planned at 46.5 percent.

ASSIGNMENT 8.3

Developing a Six-Month Buying Plan

1.

	FEB	MAR	APR	MAY	JUNE	JULY	TOTALS
Sales							
BOM							
EOM							
Reductions							

2.

	FEB	MAR	APR	MAY	JUNE	JULY	TOTALS
Sales							
BOM							
EOM							
Reductions							

3.

	FEB	MAR	APR	MAY	JUNE	JULY	TOTALS
Sales							
BOM							
EOM							
Reductions							

4.

	FEB	MAR	APR	MAY	JUNE	JULY	TOTALS
Sales							
BOM							
EOM							
Reductions							

5.

	FEB	MAR	APR	MAY	JUNE	JULY	TOTALS
Sales							
BOM							
EOM							
Reductions							

6.

	FEB	MAR	APR	MAY	JUNE	JULY	TOTALS
Sales							
BOM							
EOM							
Reductions							
Purchases (Retail)							
Purchases (Cost)							

7.

	FEB	MAR	APR	MAY	JUNE	JULY	TOTALS
Sales							
BOM							
EOM							
Reductions							
Purchases (Retail)							
Purchases (Cost)							

8.

	FEB	MAR	APR	MAY	JUNE	JULY	TOTALS
Sales							
BOM							
EOM							
Reductions							
Purchases (Retail)							
Purchases (Cost)							

9.

	FEB	MAR	APR	MAY	JUNE	JULY	TOTALS
Sales							
BOM							
EOM							
Reductions							
Purchases (Retail)							
Purchases (Cost)							

10.

	FEB	MAR	APR	MAY	JUNE	JULY	TOTALS
Sales							
BOM							
EOM							
Reductions							
Purchases (Retail)							
Purchases (Cost)							

Chapter 9

Assortment Planning

MERCHANDISING CONCEPT 9-1: CALCULATE ASSORTMENTS TO BE PURCHASED

Within any merchandise class, some varieties or styles may be more popular than others. A **_unit assortment plan_** tries to match the variety of inventory with customer needs. Assortment planning will result in establishing a **_model stock_**, which is the desired assortment of stock broken down according to selection factors important to your target market, such as brand, price, material, color, and size. The objective of establishing a model stock is to maximize the sales and profits from your inventory investment. After you have determined the budget for merchandise purchases and examined store records, trends, and external factors affecting sales, you are ready to prepare an assortment plan using the steps that follow:

Step One. Decide what general classifications of products your store or department will carry. For example, you may decide to sell men's, women's, and children's apparel. You would then divide these classifications into subclassifications. For example, men's apparel could be broken down into suits, sport coats, blazers, neckwear, and so forth. Subclassifications for home furnishings can be found in Figure 9.1.

Step Two. Determine the brands and price lines that you will carry for each of these subclassifications. Knowing characteristics of your target

FIGURE 9.1
Merchandise Classifications: Home Furnishings

Code	Subclassification
7011	Furniture and Bedding
7015	Floor Coverings
7021	China and Glassware
7025	Silverware
7031	Lamps, Pictures, and Mirrors
7035	Gifts and Christmas Decorations
7041	Major Appliances
7045	Housewares and Small Appliances
7051	Linens and Domestics
7055	Window and Furniture Coverings
7061	Notions and Closet Accessories
7065	Sewing Fabrics, Patterns, and Needlework
7091	All Other Home Furnishings

market is vital. You will need to decide on the price lines that will be most appealing to your customers.

Step Three. Identify all the general characteristics of an item that customers may consider when purchasing it. For example, sweatshirts may be available in different colors, sizes, fabrics, and styles. Men's dress shirts have different colors, sizes, sleeve lengths, and collar styles, and are made from different fabrics.

Step Four. Determine the proportion in which each selection factor will be represented in your stock. For example, not all sizes or colors will have the same rate of sale. Nor will each color be equally popular in every size that is manufactured.

Step Five. Calculate the specific number of units to purchase. As you prepare your assortment plan, carry brands for which there is adequate customer demand, and carry a complete assortment of these brands. Attempting to offer an assortment plan with too much depth in relation to your merchandise budget will result in stockouts and dissatisfied customers.

SAMPLE PROBLEM

Assume that your department is selling sweatshirts. Your investigations of past sales records indicated that sweatshirts have typically comprised 5 percent of total sales for the department. This year total sales are estimated to be $100,000. From market research you realize that most of your customers for this product are not brand loyal. They will substitute one brand for another if you have the size, color, and style for which they are looking. Past sales records indicate that Russell has been the most popular brand with your customers, and your six-month merchandise buying plan indicates that you have $5,000 to spend on sweatshirts for the coming season. If you decide to stock only Russell sweatshirts costing $10 each, you will be able to purchase 500 sweatshirts. You must then calculate the specific unit breakdowns of these shirts.

Russell has these sweatshirts in sizes from extra small to extra-extra large in 20 different colors. By examining past sales records, you determine that the size distribution of your customers has been:

Medium	20%
Large	50%
X-Large	30%

Basic colors of white and gray have been your best-sellers in the past, accounting for 40 percent of sales each. Black has been a good seller too, with 20 percent of sales.

Calculate the number of sweatshirts that you will purchase for each of the sizes and colors selected.

Sample Solution

Size	Number	Color	Number
Medium	100 (.20 × 500)	White	40 (100 × .40)
		Gray	40 (100 × .40)
		Black	20 (100 × .20)
Large	250 (.50 × 500)	White	100 (250 × .40)
		Gray	100 (250 × .40)
		Black	50 (250 × .20)
X-Large	150 (.30 × 500)	White	60 (150 × .40)
		Gray	60 (150 × .40)
		Black	30 (150 × .20)

Using Computerized Spreadsheets

You can develop assortment plans very quickly using a computerized spreadsheet. You also have the opportunity to make changes easily in your plan quickly.

1. Using you *Merchandising CD*, follow instructions you have previously used to open file **CH09-1-1**. Enter the dollar budget that is presented in the sample problem. Did you get the same assortment as shown in Figure 9.2?
2. Now develop assortment plans for the situations that follow. Record all your answers on the forms for **ASSIGNMENT 9.1.1**.
3. When you have completed the lesson, **Save** the file under the file name **CH09-1-1A**, and then **Close** the file.
4. **Quit** the spreadsheet, unless you will be completing the next assignment immediately.

FIGURE 9.2

ASSORTMENT PLANNING				
Budget	$5,000.00			
Unit Cost	$10.00			
Units Needed	500			
Size Distribution				
* Medium	0.20			
* Large	0.50			
* X-Large	0.30			
Color Distribution				
* White	0.40			
* Gray	0.40			
* Black	0.20			
Size/Color	White	Gray	Black	TOTALS
Medium	40	40	20	100
Large	100	100	50	250
X-Large	60	60	30	150
TOTALS	200	200	100	500

Assignment Problems

1. Determine the assortment plan for the sample problem if you just learned that your budget had been reduced to $4,500.
2. For the original problem (budget at $5,000), determine the assortment plan if the unit cost of each sweatshirt was increased to $12.50 each.
3. For the original problem (unit cost at $10), determine the assortment plan if you decided to change the size distribution as follows: medium (20 percent), large (40 percent), and extra-large (40 percent).
4. If the size distribution was the same as presented in the illustrative problem, determine the assortment plan if you decided to change the color distribution as follows: white (40 percent), gray (60 percent), and black (0 percent).

ASSIGNMENT 9.1.1

Developing Assortment Plans

1.

Size/Color	White	Gray	Black	TOTALS
Medium				
Large				
X-Large				

2.

Size/Color	White	Gray	Black	TOTALS
Medium				
Large				
X-Large				

3.

Size/Color	White	Gray	Black	TOTALS
Medium				
Large				
X-Large				

4.

Size/Color	White	Gray	Black	TOTALS
Medium				
Large				
X-Large				

Creating and Using Your Own Spreadsheet

1. Using your *Merchandising CD*, follow instructions you have previously used to open file **CH09-1-2**.
2. In unused cells, design your own spreadsheet to develop assortment plans for the situations that follow. Examine Figure 9.3 to view a sample layout. Record all your answers on the forms for **ASSIGNMENT 9.1.2**.
3. When you have completed the lesson, **Save** the file under the file name **CH09-1-2A**, and then **Close** the file.
4. **Quit** the spreadsheet, unless you will be completing the next assignment immediately.

FIGURE 9.3

ASSORTMENT PLANNING				
Budget				
Unit Cost				
Units Needed				
Size Distribution				
* Small				
* Medium				
* Large				
* X-Large				
Color Distribution				
* Red				
* Blue				
* White				
* Black				
Size/Color	Red	Blue	White	Black
Small				
Medium				
Large				
X-Large				
TOTALS				

Assignment Problems

1. You have the budget to purchase 100 sweatshirts for your store. All the sweatshirts will be purchased from Hanes for $12 each. The distribution of sizes will be as follows:

Small	20%
Medium	28%
Large	32%
X-Large	20%

    Four colors will be represented in the assortment as follows:

Red	25%
Blue	25%
White	25%
Black	25%

    Develop an assortment plan based on this information. Then, analyze the completed assortment plan. Is this an appropriate distribution for the assortment plan? If not, how could the distribution be improved?

2. Recalculate the assortment plan for the information presented in problem 1 if the distribution in sizes were changed as follows:

Small	25%
Medium	25%
Large	30%
X-Large	20%

3. Recalculate the assortment plan for the information presented in problem 1 if the distribution in colors were changed as follows:

Red	30%
Blue	30%
White	20%
Black	20%

4. Recalculate the assortment plan for the information presented in problem 1 if the distribution in colors were changed as follows:

Red	20%
Blue	20%
White	30%
Black	30%

5. Recalculate the assortment plan for the information presented in problem 1 if the distribution in sizes were changed as follows:

Small	15%
Medium	35%
Large	25%
X-Large	25%

6. You are the buyer for men's shirts at a local department store. You want to purchase short-sleeve, solid-color, 100 percent cotton shirts from two vendors (Gant and Arrow). You have a $20,000 budget, which will be distributed as follows–Gant, 75 percent; Arrow, 25 percent. Each Gant shirt will cost $15.00, while each Arrow shirt will cost $21.00.

Colors will be distributed in the following manner with both vendors:

White	70%
Blue	30%

All colors will be purchased in the following size distribution:

Small	10%
Medium	50%
Large	40%

Based on the information provided, develop an assortment plan. (*Hint*: You will need to develop a formula that will calculate total number of shirts that can be purchased from each vendor based on the planned budget.)

ASSIGNMENT 9.1.2

Developing Assortment Plans

1.

Size/Color	Red	Blue	White	Black	TOTALS
Small					
Medium					
Large					
X-Large					

2.

Size/Color	Red	Blue	White	Black	TOTALS
Small					
Medium					
Large					
X-Large					

3.

Size/Color	Red	Blue	White	Black	TOTALS
Small					
Medium					
Large					
X-Large					

4.

Size/Color	Red	Blue	White	Black	TOTALS
Small					
Medium					
Large					
X-Large					

5.

Size/Color	Red	Blue	White	Black	TOTALS
Small					
Medium					
Large					
X-Large					

6.

VENDOR: Gant			
Size/Color	White	Blue	TOTALS
Small			
Medium			
Large			
VENDOR: Arrow			
Size/Color	White	Blue	TOTALS
Small			
Medium			
Large			

Purchase Orders

MERCHANDISING CONCEPT 10–1: CALCULATE COST AND RETAIL EXTENSIONS WITH MARKUP PERCENTAGES

After buyers make the decision to purchase merchandise and negotiate terms and conditions of the sale, they are ready to complete the purchase order. The ***purchase order*** is the contract between a buyer and a vendor and must be completed carefully to avoid any costly mistakes. Today, many buyers use computer systems that allow them to electronically produce completed purchase orders. But all buyers can construct a computerized spreadsheet that will allow them to perform all the mathematical calculations they need to ensure accuracy.

Key calculations for purchase orders that buyers usually perform include:

- Cost extensions.
- Retail extensions.
- Total cost of items purchased.
- Total retail of items purchased.
- Individual markup percentages.
- Cumulative markup percentage of purchases.

A buyer is writing a purchase order to Acme Inc. for the following two items:

1. 60 shirts that cost $12.99 each and will retail for $26.50 each.
2. 20 belts that cost $7.24 each and will retail for $14.99 each.

Calculate the total cost of the purchase from Acme Inc. as well as the total retail value of the purchase. In addition, calculate the individual markup percentage on each item as well as the cumulative markup percentage on the total purchase.
Sample Solution

Step 1. Find the total cost of the purchase by multiplying the number of items purchased by the unit cost.

Item	# of Items		Unit Cost		Total Cost
Shirts	60	×	$12.99	=	$779.40
Belts	20	×	$7.24	=	$144.80
Total Cost of Purchases				=	$924.20

Step 2. Find the total retail value of the purchase by multiplying the number of items purchased by the unit retail and adding the retail value of all items purchased.

Item	# of Items		Unit Retail		Total Retail
Shirts	60	×	$26.50	=	$1,590.00
Belts	20	×	$14.99	=	$299.80
Total Retail of Purchases				=	$1,889.80

Step 3. Find the individual markup percentage for each item by dividing the dollar markup by the retail price.

Shirts ($26.50 − $12.99)/$26.50 = 51.0%
Belts ($14.99 − $7.24)/$14.99 = 51.7%

Step 4. Find the total cumulative markup percentage on the entire purchase by dividing total markup in dollars by the total retail of the purchases:

($1,889.80 − $924.20)/$1,889.80 = 51.1% (cumulative markup)

Using Computerized Spreadsheets

A spreadsheet can be constructed to perform all these calculations when the buyer enters these three pieces of information for each item purchased: (1) number of items ordered, (2) unit cost, and (3) unit retail.

1. Using your *Merchandising CD*, follow instructions you have previously used to open file **CH010-1-1**.
2. Use the spreadsheet that has already been designed to complete the problems that follow. Record all your answers on the forms for **ASSIGNMENT 10.1.1**.
3. When you have completed the lesson, **Save** the file under the file name **CH10-1-1A**, and then **Close** the file.
4. **Quit** the spreadsheet, unless you will be completing the next assignment immediately.

Assignment Problems

For each of the following problems, calculate (1) total cost of items purchased, (2) total retail value of items purchased, (3) individual markup percentages, and (4) cumulative markup percentage of purchases.

1. A buyer is writing a purchase order to Acme Inc. for the following two items:
   a. 160 shirts that cost $12.99 each and will retail for $26.50 each.
   b. 120 belts that cost $7.24 each and will retail for $14.99 each.
2. A buyer is writing a purchase order to Acme Inc. for the following two items:
   a. 58 blue jackets that cost $22.00 each and will retail for $43.99 each.
   b. 58 white blouses that cost $9.27 each and will retail for $17.99 each.
3. A buyer is writing a purchase order to Acme Inc. for the following two items:
   a. 100 pairs of men's black socks that cost $.99 a pair and will retail for $1.98 a pair.
   b. 200 pairs of men's navy blue socks that cost $.94 a pair and will retail for $1.98 a pair.
4. A buyer is writing a purchase order to Acme Inc. for the following two items:
   a. 75 scarves that cost $9.92 each and will retail for $19.50 each.
   b. 50 men's ties that cost $12.44 each and will retail for $25.00 each.

5. A buyer is writing a purchase order to Acme Inc. for the following two items:
   a. 20 raincoats that cost $41.23 each and will retail for $84.99 each.
   b. 150 pairs of gloves that cost $14.83 a pair and will retail for $29.99 a pair.

ASSIGNMENT 10.1.1

Calculating Purchase Orders

1.

Item	Total Cost	Total Retail	Markup Percentage
TOTALS			

2.

Item	Total Cost	Total Retail	Markup Percentage
TOTALS			

3.

Item	Total Cost	Total Retail	Markup Percentage
TOTALS			

4.

Item	Total Cost	Total Retail	Markup Percentage
TOTALS			

5.

Item	Total Cost	Total Retail	Markup Percentage
TOTALS			

Creating and Using Your Own Spreadsheet

The spreadsheet that you have been using will perform calculations for only one or two different items. As you probably already realize, spreadsheets can be designed to handle any number of items.

1. Using your *Merchandising CD*, follow instructions you have previously used to open file **CH10-1-2**. Design a spreadsheet that will perform the following calculations for five different items:
   - Cost extensions for each item.
   - Retail extensions for each item.
   - Total cost of all items purchased.
   - Total retail value of all items purchased.
   - Individual markup percentages.
   - Cumulative markup percentage of purchases.

   As in the purchase order problems you have already worked, cells should be designated for entering the number of each item purchased, as well as the unit cost and unit retail for each item.

2. Enter your titles before setting up your formulas. When you have finished, your spreadsheet layout should resemble the one shown in Figure 10.1.

3. Use your spreadsheet to answer the problems that follow. For each problem, calculate the following:
   - Total cost of items purchased.
   - Total retail value of items purchased.
   - Individual markup percentages.
   - Cumulative markup percentage of purchases.

   Record all your answers on the forms for **ASSIGNMENT 10.1.2**.

FIGURE 10.1

PURCHASE ORDERS						
	Units	Unit Cost	Unit Retail	Total Cost	Total Retail	Markup %
Product 1				$0.00	$0.00	#DIV/0!
Product 2				$0.00	$0.00	#DIV/0!
Product 3				$0.00	$0.00	#DIV/0!
Product 4				$0.00	$0.00	#DIV/0!
Product 5				$0.00	$0.00	#DIV/0!
TOTALS				$0.00	$0.00	#DIV/0!

4. When you have completed the lesson, **Save** the file under the file name **CH10-1-2A**, and then **Close** the file.

5. **Quit** the spreadsheet, unless you will be completing the next assignment immediately.

Assignment Problems

1.

Stock #	Units Orders	Unit Cost	Unit Retail
1234	288	$1.23	$2.50
1235	50	$26.98	$55.99
1236	24	$99.00	$199.99
1237	124	$21.45	$39.99
1238	10	$82.45	$175.99

2.

Stock #	Units Orders	Unit Cost	Unit Retail
1234	88	$1.23	$2.50
1235	10	$26.98	$55.99
1236	14	$99.00	$199.99
1237	24	$21.45	$39.99
1238	15	$82.45	$175.99

3.

Stock #	Units Orders	Unit Cost	Unit Retail
1234	288	$1.40	$2.50
1235	50	$26.00	$55.99
1236	24	$99.99	$199.99
1237	124	$21.00	$39.99
1238	10	$82.00	$175.99

4.

Stock #	Units Orders	Unit Cost	Unit Retail
1234	288	$1.23	$2.99
1235	50	$26.98	$56.99
1236	24	$99.00	$199.99
1237	124	$21.45	$40.99
1238	10	$82.45	$176.99

5.

Stock #	Units Orders	Unit Cost	Unit Retail
1234	1,288	$11.23	$22.50
1235	150	$26.98	$55.99
1236	124	$99.00	$199.99
1237	1,124	$21.45	$39.99
1238	110	$82.45	$175.99

ASSIGNMENT 10.1.2

Calculating Purchase Orders

1.

Item	Total Cost	Total Retail	Markup Percentage
TOTALS			

2.

Item	Total Cost	Total Retail	Markup Percentage
TOTALS			

3.

Item	Total Cost	Total Retail	Markup Percentage
TOTALS			

4.

Item	Total Cost	Total Retail	Markup Percentage
TOTALS			

5.

Item	Total Cost	Total Retail	Markup Percentage
TOTALS			

Open-to-Buy

MERCHANDISING CONCEPT 11–1: CALCULATE OPEN-TO-BUY

For the six-month merchandise plan that you developed in Chapter 8, the dollar amount of purchases that were to be made each month was calculated. However, not all the required monthly stock is purchased at the beginning of the month. Purchase decisions are distributed throughout the month in order to take advantage of new merchandise lines, to reorder fast-selling merchandise, or to acquire off-price merchandise to use in promotional sales. Moreover, buyers may have outstanding orders—commitments to vendors that have not been delivered. The value of these outstanding orders will reduce the planned purchases for the month. As a result, buyers must be able to calculate, on a specific date during the month, the amount of merchandise to be purchased during the remainder of the month. The remaining purchases are defined as open-to-buy. **Open-to-buy** is the amount the buyer has left to spend for a period and is reduced each time a purchase is made. It is calculated using the following formula:

Open-to-Buy = Planned Purchases − Merchandise on Order

When a negative number results from this calculation, buyers are in an **overbought** position. In other words, they have no open-to-buy; they have already made too many purchases above their plan, or other estimates (such as sales or reductions) were inaccurate.

SAMPLE PROBLEM

For the month of February, purchases of $22,000 (at retail) are planned. Merchandise already on order amounts to $11,455. Calculate open-to-buy.

Sample Solution

Open-to-Buy = Planned Purchases − Merchandise on Order
Open-to-Buy = $22,000 − $11,455
Open-to-Buy = $10,545

The buyer still has $10,545 (at retail) to spend during the month of February. Most buyers will want to calculate open-to-buy at cost so that they will know exactly how many dollars they have to spend. Open-to-buy (at cost) can be calculated by multiplying retail dollars times (100% − Initial Markup Percentage) as follows:

Open-to-Buy (at Cost) = Open-to-Buy (at Retail) × (100% − Initial Markup %)

For example, if the initial markup percentage had been 45 percent in the preceding situation, open-to-buy (at cost) could be calculated as follows:

Open-to-Buy (at Cost) = Open-to-Buy (at Retail)
          × (100% − Initial Markup %)
Open-to-Buy (at Cost) = $10,545 × (100% − 45%)
Open-to-Buy (at Cost) = $10,545 × .55
Open-to-Buy (at Cost) = $5,799.75

Using Computerized Spreadsheets

1. Using your *Merchandising CD*, follow instructions you have previously used to open file **CH11-1-1**. Input the information from the illustrative problem.
2. Use the spreadsheet to calculate open-to-buy at both cost and retail for the questions that follow. Record all your answers on the form for **ASSIGNMENT 11.1.1**.
3. When you have completed the lesson, **Save** the file under the file name **CH11-1-1A**, and then **Close** the file.

4. **Quit** the spreadsheet, unless you will be completing the next assignment immediately.

Assignment Problems

A buyer has planned purchases for the month of March for the ten items listed below. At the end of the first week in March, the buyer wants to determine the open-to-buy (at both retail and cost) for each of these items. Initial markup percentages as well as purchases to date are provided for each item. Calculate open-to-buy (at both retail and cost).

	Planned Purchases (at Retail)	Purchases to Date	Initial Markup %
1.	$14,900	$10,500	49.5%
2.	$27,400	$17,900	49.0%
3.	$11,800	$10,500	47.5%
4.	$9,700	$9,000	49.5%
5.	$15,300	$10,700	49.0%
6.	$12,900	$13,000	49.0%
7.	$19,100	$19,000	49.5%
8.	$14,300	$1,500	49.5%
9.	$9,200	$9,000	49.0%
10.	$1,300	$1,250	49.5%

ASSIGNMENT 11.1.1

Calculating Open-to-Buy

Problem	Open-to-Buy (at Retail)	Open-to-Buy (at Cost)
1.		
2.		
3.		
4.		
5.		
6.		
7.		
8.		
9.		
10.		

FIGURE 11.1

OPEN-TO-BUY	
Initial Markup %	
Planned Purchases at Retail	
On Order	
On Order	
On Order	
Open-to-Buy (at Retail)	$0.00
Open-to-Buy (at Cost)	$0.00

Creating and Using Your Own Spreadsheet

Many times, buyers will have more than one outstanding order for a product classification or department.

1. Using your *Merchandising CD*, follow instructions you have previously used to open file **CH11-1-2**. Design a spreadsheet calculation that will allow you to calculate open-to-buy at cost when there are up to three outstanding orders.
2. Type your titles; then design formulas that will allow you to calculate open-to-buy at both retail and cost when up to three purchases are on order. Your completed spreadsheet layout should resemble the one shown in Figure 11.1.
3. Use your spreadsheet to calculate open-to-buy at both retail and cost for the problems that follow. Record all your answers on the form for **ASSIGNMENT 11.1.2**.
4. When you have completed the lesson, **Save** the file under the file name **CH11-1-2A**, and then **Close** the file.
5. **Quit** the spreadsheet, unless you will be completing the next assignment immediately.

Assignment Problems

1. Planned purchases for stock number 12789 are $43,200 (at retail). Purchases are on order from three vendors in these amounts—vendor 1, $11,500; vendor 2, $12,400, and vendor 3, $15,000. If the initial markup is 44.6 percent, calculate open-to-buy at both retail and cost.

2. Planned purchases for stock number 12889 are $43,200 (at retail). Purchases are on order from three vendors in these amounts—vendor 1, $21,500; vendor 2, $14,400, and vendor 3, $9,000. If the initial markup is 49.6 percent, calculate open-to-buy at both retail and cost.

3. Planned purchases for stock number 12689 are $23,200 (at retail). Purchases are on order from three vendors in these amounts—vendor 1, $1,500; vendor 2, $2,400, and vendor 3, $15,000. If the initial markup is 48.6 percent, calculate open-to-buy at both retail and cost.

4. Planned purchases for stock number 12589 are $33,000 (at retail). Purchases are on order from three vendors in these amounts—vendor 1, $10,500; vendor 2, $10,400, and vendor 3, $10,000. If the initial markup is 44.6 percent, calculate open-to-buy at both retail and cost.

5. Planned purchases for stock number 12489 are $3,200 (at retail). Purchases are on order from three vendors in these amounts—vendor 1, $1,500; vendor 2, $500, and vendor 3, $1,000. If the initial markup is 44.6 percent, calculate open-to-buy at both retail and cost.

ASSIGNMENT 11.1.2

Calculating Open-to-Buy

Problem	Open-to-Buy (at Retail)	Open-to-Buy (at Cost)
1.		
2.		
3.		
4.		
5.		

Operating Results

MERCHANDISING CONCEPT 12–1: CALCULATE PROFIT OR LOSS

Buyers and merchandisers should know how profit is calculated because the decisions they make determine how profitable the store will be. Typically, profit calculations are shown on an operating statement, also known as a ***profit or loss statement*** or ***income statement***. Key components of this form include the following:

- ***Net sales*** represent the real volume of sales that have occurred. In other words, net sales equal total sales minus returns made by customers or allowances granted to customers.
- ***Cost of goods sold*** represents the actual cost of the merchandise that was sold during the month.
- ***Gross margin*** is the difference between the cost of goods sold and net sales. It represents money remaining to cover the store's operating expenses.
- ***Operating expenses*** are expenses incurred in operating the business. Salaries, rent, advertising, and utilities would be operating expenses. The cost of the merchandise sold is not an operating expense.
- ***Profit*** is the amount of money that remains after operating expenses have been subtracted from gross margin. If the operating expenses of a business are greater than gross margin, a loss results.

These are the five basic components of an ***operating statement*** for a business. Detailed operating statements contain much more information; however, most buyers and merchandisers make decisions that affect only net sales and cost of goods sold. Store management controls operating expenses that also will affect whether the store makes a profit or a loss.

Usually, the operating statement will contain both dollar amounts and percentages. Percentages are used because they can be compared more easily than dollar figures. The use of percentages also helps to show the distribution of the sales dollars among the various elements of the operating statement.

When converting dollar amounts on the operating statement to percentages, the net sales amount always equals 100 percent. The percentage of net sales that each component of the operating statement represents is determined by dividing by the dollar amount of net sales.

The total of all the sales made during a period is called ***gross sales***. The returns received from customers or allowances granted them because of defective merchandise are deducted from gross sales. These deductions are called ***returns and allowances***. They are important to management because they might be indicators of high-pressure selling or poor-quality merchandise. They also represent additional selling expenses because the returned merchandise may have to be marked down. When returns and allowances are subtracted from gross sales, the net sales figures is obtained. This figure is expressed in the following formula:

Net Sales = Gross Sales − Customer Returns and Allowances

Likewise, determining cost of goods sold requires additional calculations. The calculation starts with the opening or beginning inventory figure that represents the cost of merchandise on hand at the start of the operating period. To this figure is added the cost of all purchases made during the period. Also added to this figure are inward freight charges and the cost of any alterations/workroom costs. The dollar amount of any discounts is subtracted along with the cost of the closing or ending inventory. The result is cost of goods sold.

In the problems related to operating statements that you have already completed, totals for net sales, cost of goods, and expenses were given in the problem. However, each of these components of the operating statement can be calculated using computerized spreadsheets.

SAMPLE PROBLEM

During the year, net sales for a florist were $200,000. Cost of goods sold was $105,000, and operating expenses totaled $75,000. Complete an operating statement, showing both dollar amounts and percentages.

Sample Solution

First, substitute into the operating statement the information you already know, as follows:

Net Sales	$200,000
− Cost of Goods Sold	−$105,000
= **Gross Margin**	=_____
− Operating Expenses	− $75,000
= **Profit**	=_____

Next, gross margin can be determined by subtracting cost of goods sold from net sales; therefore, gross margin equals $95,000 ($200,000 − $105,000). Then, profit can be calculated by subtracting operating expenses from gross margin. In this situation, profit would equal $20,000 ($95,000 − $75,000).

Now, you need to convert these dollar amounts to percentages as follows:

Net Sales	100.0%
Cost of Goods Sold	52.5% (calculated by $105,000/$200,000)
Gross Margin	47.5% (calculated by $95,000/$200,000)
Operating Expenses	37.5% (calculated by $75,000/$200,000)
Profit	10.0% (calculated by $20,000/$200,000)

Remember, that the net sales percentage will always equal 100 percent, and other percentages are found by dividing the dollar amount for that component by the dollar amount of net sales.

Using Computerized Spreadsheets

1. Using your *Merchandising CD*, follow instructions you have previously used to open file **CH12-1-1**.
2. Use the spreadsheet that has already been prepared to calculate the components of an operating statement *as a dollar amount and as a percentage* for the problems that follow. Record all your answers on the forms for **ASSIGNMENT 12.1.1**.

3. When you have completed the lesson, **Save** the file under the file name **CH12-1-1A**, and then **Close** the file.
4. **Quit** the spreadsheet, unless you will be completing the next assignment immediately.

Assignment Problems

1. The swimwear department has the following figures available: Sales were $135,000; cost of goods sold was $120,000; and operating expenses were $11,500.
2. ABC department has the following figures available: Sales were $110,000; cost of goods sold was $80,000; and operating expenses were $35,000.
3. A department had sales of $300,000. Cost of goods sold was $180,000; and operating expenses were $90,500.
4. A store has the following figures available: Sales were $278,000; cost of goods sold was $190,000; and operating expenses were $78,500.
5. A convenience store had net sales of $495,000, with the cost of goods sold at $250,000. Operating expenses totaled $198,568.

ASSIGNMENT 12.1.1
Calculating Components of Operating Statements

1.

	$ (Dollars)	% (Percentages)
Net Sales		
Cost of Goods Sold		
Gross Margin		
Operating Expenses		
Profit		

2.

	$ (Dollars)	% (Percentages)
Net Sales		
Cost of Goods Sold		
Gross Margin		
Operating Expenses		
Profit		

3.

	$ (Dollars)	% (Percentages)
Net Sales		
Cost of Goods Sold		
Gross Margin		
Operating Expenses		
Profit		

4.

	$ (Dollars)	% (Percentages)
Net Sales		
Cost of Goods Sold		
Gross Margin		
Operating Expenses		
Profit		

5.

	$ (Dollars)	% (Percentages)
Net Sales		
Cost of Goods Sold		
Gross Margin		
Operating Expenses		
Profit		

Creating and Using Your Own Spreadsheet

1. Using your *Merchandising CD*, follow instructions you have previously used to open file **CH12-1-2**. Type the following titles:

   - **Gross Sales**
   - **Customer Returns**
   - **BOM**
   - **Purchases**
   - **Freight**
   - **Workroom Costs**
   - **Cash Discounts**
   - **EOM**
   - **Fixed Expenses**
   - **Variable Expenses**

   You should be able to enter numerical data in the cells to the right of each of these titles.

2. Next, type the following titles

  • **Net Sales**
  • **Cost of Goods Sold**
  • **Gross Margin**
  • **Expenses**
  • **Profit**

  To the right of each of these titles enter the formula that will allow you to calculate each component (as a dollar amount and as a percentage) based on the cell addresses of the needed data. Your completed spreadsheet layout should resemble the one shown in Figure 12.1.

3. Once you have entered all your titles and formulas, use your spreadsheet to complete the problems that follow. Record all your answers on the forms for **ASSIGNMENT 12.1.2**.

4. When you have completed the lesson, **Save** the file under the file name **CH12-1-2A**, and then **Close** the file.

5. **Quit** the spreadsheet, unless you will be completing the next assignment immediately.

FIGURE 12.1

OPERATING RESULTS		
Gross Sales		
Customer Returns		
BOM		
Purchases		
Freight		
Workroom Costs		
Cash Discounts		
EOM		
Fixed Expenses		
Variable Expenses		
	Dollars	**Percentages**
Net Sales		
Cost of Goods Sold		
Gross Margin		
Expenses		
Profit		

Assignment Problems

1. Based on the information that follows, calculate the components of an operating statement as a dollar amount and as a percentage.

Gross Sales	$125,000
Customer Returns	$4,500
Cost of Beginning Inventory	$30,000
Cost of Ending Inventory	$32,000
Fixed Expenses	$43,000
Variable Expenses	$10,000
Purchases (at Cost)	$60,000
Freight	$900
Cash Discounts	$7,500

2. Based on the information that follows, calculate the components of an operating statement as a dollar amount and as a percentage.

Gross Sales	$180,000
Customer Returns	$8,500
Cost of Beginning Inventory	$39,000
Cost of Ending Inventory	$45,000
Fixed Expenses	$52,000
Variable Expenses	$26,000
Purchases (at Cost)	$94,000
Freight	$900
Cash Discounts	$7,500
Alteration/Workroom Expenses	$950

3. Based on the information that follows, calculate the components of an operating statement as a dollar amount and as a percentage.

Gross Sales	$175,000
Customer Returns	$8,500
Cost of Beginning Inventory	$30,000
Cost of Ending Inventory	$31,000
Fixed Expenses	$35,000
Variable Expenses	$30,000
Purchases (at Cost)	$90,000
Freight	$900
Cash Discounts	$6,500

4. Based on the information that follows, calculate the components of an operating statement as a dollar amount and as a percentage.

Gross Sales	$105,000
Customer Returns	$3,500
Cost of Beginning Inventory	$29,000
Cost of Ending Inventory	$31,000
Fixed Expenses	$17,000
Variable Expenses	$21,000
Purchases (at Cost)	$49,000
Freight	$900
Cash Discounts	$7,500
Alteration/Workroom Expenses	$1,000

5. Based on the information that follows, calculate the components of an operating statement as a dollar amount and as a percentage.

Gross Sales	$130,000
Customer Returns	$5,500
Cost of Beginning Inventory	$35,000
Cost of Ending Inventory	$37,000
Fixed Expenses	$45,000
Variable Expenses	$11,000
Purchases (at Cost)	$65,000
Freight	$900

ASSIGNMENT 12.1.2
Calculating Components of Operating Statements

1.

	$ (Dollars)	% (Percentages)
Net Sales		
Cost of Goods Sold		
Gross Margin		
Operating Expenses		
Profit		

2.

	$ (Dollars)	% (Percentages)
Net Sales		
Cost of Goods Sold		
Gross Margin		
Operating Expenses		
Profit		

3.

	$ (Dollars)	% (Percentages)
Net Sales		
Cost of Goods Sold		
Gross Margin		
Operating Expenses		
Profit		

4.

	$ (Dollars)	% (Percentages)
Net Sales		
Cost of Goods Sold		
Gross Margin		
Operating Expenses		
Profit		

5.

	$ (Dollars)	% (Percentages)
Net Sales		
Cost of Goods Sold		
Gross Margin		
Operating Expenses		
Profit		

Glossary

alteration/workroom expenses Expenses that occur when retailers make changes in their merchandise to satisfy special customer needs (i.e., clothing alterations or engravings); treated as part of cost of goods sold

cash discounts Discounts granted to retailers for early payment of invoices

cell address Location identifier for a cell; determined by row and column location; shown on the bottom status line of the computer screen.

cells Small rectangular subdivisions of a spreadsheet

column A vertical series of cells in a spreadsheet

cost of goods sold (COGS) Includes the actual cost of the merchandise purchased plus freight charges and any alteration/workroom expenses; any cash discounts would also be subtracted

cumulative markup Markup achieved on all merchandise available for sale in a given period

discounts Reductions in retail price

functions Abbreviated formulas that perform a specific operation on a group of variables

gross margin Sales revenue that remains after cost of goods sold has been deducted

gross sales Total of all sales made during any period of time

highlight bar Shaded marker on the computer screen that identifies the current cell

income statement A business report which shows profit calculations

individual markup The markup on one item of merchandise

initial markup The first markup placed on merchandise when it arrives in the store

maintained markup The markup that is actually realized after the merchandise is sold

markdown Reductions in the retail price of merchandise

markdown cancellation Increases in the retail price to offset all or any part of previously taken markdowns; usually occurs when a markdown has been temporarily taken for promotional purposes

markup The amount added to the cost of goods to determine the retail price

markup percentage The markup in dollars divided by the retail price

model stock The desired merchandise assortment broken down according to the selection factors important to the store's customers

net sales Calculated by subtracting customer returns and allowances from gross sales

off-retail percentage Calculated by dividing the dollar amount of markdown by the original retail price

open-to-buy (OTB) The amount of money that the buyer has left to spend for a period

operating expenses All the expenses incurred in operating a business, both fixed and variable

operating statement A report that shows the profit or loss calculations for a store or department; also called an income statement

overbought A condition in which buyers have purchased more than they planned during a specific period of time

planned purchases The dollar amount of merchandise a buyer plans to purchase during a period of time

profit The amount of money remaining after operating expenses have been subtracted from gross margin

profit or loss statement A business report which shows profit calculations.

purchase order The contract between the buyer and the seller for the purchase of merchandise

reductions Includes markdowns, employee and consumer discounts, and inventory shortages

returns and allowances Includes merchandise returned by customers or allowances granted them because of defective merchandise; subtracted from gross sales to calculate net sales

row A horizontal series of cells on a spreadsheet

shortages Merchandise disappearance that has occurred due to shoplifting, employee theft, or paperwork errors

six-month merchandise buying plan A tool used by retailers to translate profit objectives into a six-month framework for merchandise planning and control

spreadsheet A computerized electronic worksheet that performs mathematical calculations

stock-to-sales ratio method A method of stock planning that involves maintaining inventory in a specific ratio to sales

stock turnover rate Relates to the number of times that the average stock is sold during a given period of time

unit assortment plan Represents the merchandise buying plan that has been translated to specific pieces of merchandise (i.e., color, size, or model)

Appendix

BASIC RETAIL MATH FORMULAS

Pricing Calculations

Retail = Cost/(100% − Markup %)

Cost = Retail × (100% − Markup %)

Markup % = (Retail − Cost)/Retail

Initial Markup % = (Expenses + Profit + Reductions + Alteration or Workroom Expenses − Cash Discounts)/(Sales + Reductions)

Repricing Calculations

$ Markdown = (Original Retail Price − Sale Price) × Number of Items Reduced

Markdown % = Total $ Markdown/$ Net Sales

Off-Retail % = Dollar Markdown/Original Retail Price

Markdown Cancellation = (New Retail Price − Sale Price) × Number of Items Repriced

Maintained Markup % = Initial Markup % − [Reductions % × (100% − Initial Markup %)]

Stock Planning Calculations

Stock Turnover Rate = Sales/Average Stock
Sales = Stock Turnover Rate × Average Stock
Average Stock = Sales/Stock Turnover Rate
Stock-to-Sales Ratio = Value of Stock/Actual Sales
BOM Stock = Stock-to-Sales Ratio × Planned Sales

Merchandise Planning Calculations

Planned Purchases (at Retail) = Planned Sales + Planned Reductions + Planned EOM − Planned BOM
Planned Purchases (at Cost) = Planned Purchases [at Retail] × (100% − Markup %]
Open-to-Buy = Planned Purchases − Merchandise on Order
Open-to-Buy (at Cost) = Open-to-Buy (at Retail) × (100% − Markup %)

Profit Calculations

Net Sales = Gross Sales − Customer Returns and Allowances
Cost of Goods Sold = Beginning Inventory + Purchases + Freight Charges + Alteration or Workroom Expenses − Cash Discounts
Gross Margin = Net Sales − Cost of Goods Sold
Profit = Gross Margin − Operating Expenses
Profit % = $ Profit/Net Sales

Index